The Toolbox

for Remodeling Your Problem Dog

The Toolbox

for Remodeling Your Problem Dog

by Terry Ryan

Drawings by
Jackie McCowen

Howell Book House

New York

Howell Book House
A Simon & Schuster Macmillan Company
1633 Broadway
New York, NY 10019-6785

Macmillan Publishing books may be purchased for business or sales promotional use.
For information please write: Special Markets Department, Macmillan Publishing USA,
1633 Broadway, New York, NY 10019-6785.

Library of Congress Cataloging-in-Publication
Ryan, Terry (Theresa Diana)
   The toolbox for remodeling your problem dog / by Terry Ryan :
drawings by Jackie McGowan.
      p.   cm.
   Includes index.
   ISBN 0-87605-049-6
   1. Dogs—Training.   2. Dogs—Behavior.   I. Title.
   SF431.R935   1997
   636.7'088'7—dc21   97-30072
                                                                       CIP

Manufactured in the United States of America
00 99 98 — 10 9 8 7 6 5 4 3 2 1

Book design by A & D Howell Design
Cover Design by DesignLab

Dedication

For Bill, Jenn and Kyle, the human family that has accompanied me along my many doggy digressions.

Table of Contents

Foreword

When you read Terry Ryan's suggestions on how to raise a dog and how to train it, her ideas seem so logical, so sensible, that you might think she's just parroting what's been said for decades. Not so. The concept of training dogs to behave the way we want them to behave *because they want to behave that way* is surprisingly new.

There has always been a bit of the "guy" thing about dog training. Historically, training dogs to work to the gun, to herd or to guard livestock, or to protect property was a man's job. In this century, for many dog owners the epitome of the well-trained dog is the German Shepherd Dog. On television, in films, and in real life, the ever obedient, always faithful and well-trained Shepherd guides blind people, tracks and rescues lost people, or defends property from nasty people. The German Shepherd Dog was originally bred by military men and trained by military men who used military methods to ensure canine compliance. The trainer was the harsh sergeant-major, and the dog the obedient private. Disobedience was corrected through rigid discipline.

That system works. Like horses, dogs are "broken" to the will of the trainer. Out of fear of the consequences, they perform as required. It's a logical, masculine way of thinking. Today, however, with a more sophisticated understanding of both our own behavior and canine behavior, the system of training dogs by forced compliance has changed to training through rewards for doing well. From as early an age as is practical, the dog's personality and behavior is molded by reinforcing good behavior.

This is a more subtle, sophisticated approach to training, and it was a guy—the English-trained, California-based veterinarian Ian Dunbar—who, in the late 1960s, developed the concept of "positive reinforcement" dog training. Train dogs to do what we want dogs to do because the dogs actually want to do it. This demands a good understanding of the dog's mind—what motivates his or her behavior. Call me sexist, but this is something that a typical woman's mind is probably better at understanding than a typical man's.

Starting in the early 1970s, Terry Ryan took this concept and fine-tuned it into the refreshing ideas she explains in this book. Throughout the United States and

Canada, but also in Europe and especially Australia and Japan, she introduced her dog training ideas to other dog trainers in "master classes." She is a trainer's trainer.

If you follow Terry's suggestions, both you and your dog will find training a pleasure. Guaranteed. It's also personally satisfying to see how rewarding good behavior is such a successful training method. And once you've tested her training methods with your dog, you might even want to try them on the kids.

Good luck.

Bruce Fogle, DVM, MRCVS

Introduction

Always a dog lover, I started teaching dog obedience classes in 1972. I followed a lesson plan and used techniques that had been in existence, unchanged, for many years. While a fine organization, the training club where I taught was like most clubs of that era, providing pet owners with a rigid, unyielding curriculum. It did not take me long to discover that not every student fit into the club's pigeonhole.

When I moved on to design and teach my own classes, I made it a policy to record profiles on all incoming students. The answer to one of my questions, "Why did you come to class?" defined the evolution of my class curriculum from traditional dog obedience exercises to behavior and training classes. In filling out the profiles, students typically reported the desire to get their dogs to stop doing something: stop jumping up on visitors, stop destroying the house, stop running away, stop barking, stop digging. Stop! My classes helped people to train dogs to *do* something, not to *stop* doing something.

At last the light came on. If I really wanted to make a difference, if I really wanted to help, I needed to design a practical program that effectively addressed the real concerns of the pet owner.

Each dog and owner team is different. The combinations of independent variables are endless. Drawing a blueprint for success that meets everyone's needs is near to impossible. But I can give you a set of tools and an explanation of how to use them to build a training program that is right for you and your dog.

Foundation Blocks

The First Foundation Stone: Educating the Builder

It's my guess that you picked up this book because of one word on the cover: *problem.* Webster's defines the word *problem* as "very difficult to train or discipline: as, a *problem* child."

Does this describe your dog? As you work through this book, you'll learn that there are very few problem dogs in the true sense of the word. Mostly we have normal dogs doing normal doggy things, but at the wrong place or time for their owner's lifestyle.

You may be anxious to change some of your pal's inappropriate behavior, but first let's explore canine behavior in general and how the environment you provide for your dog affects your dog's actions.

Someone once said to me in regard to training his dog, "I just want to get into the driver's seat and drive; I don't want to know the internal workings of the combustion engine." My philosophy on dog training is more empirical in nature. Just learning how to drive might be OK, until something unusual happens, something goes wrong that is beyond simply turning the key and stepping on the gas pedal. You need to look at the big picture. Let's try to understand the inner workings of your dog before you get into the driver's seat.

Popular literature traces the modern dog's evolution from *Canis lupus* (the wolf) through to *Canis familiarus* (the pet dog). But a new species has evolved, and it's the one I'm most concerned with: ***Canis obnoxious!***

Most dogs don't deserve this label. Let's take a look at why dogs are misunderstood, mismanaged and mislabeled by exploring just how they learn obnoxious behavior—or any behavior for that matter.

DOGS LEARN BY ASSOCIATION

The Law of Effect is a term coined in the early 1900s by researchers interested in the principles of learning and behavior. Paraphrased, the law states: If a response is followed by a satisfying state of affairs, that response is apt to be repeated. This concept eventually came to be known as operant conditioning. Many of the techniques in this book are based on the principles of operant conditioning.

Operant conditioning takes place all the time, even when we don't intend it. Your dog is destined to learn and is learning right now, without trying, without your help. It's easy to find examples of how dogs learn from the consequences of their behavior.

Ginger Gets Into the Trash

While you're at work, Ginger tips over the kitchen trash container. She finds a delicious steak bone. The Law of Effect is in force. The bone is her reward, and Ginger's trash-tipping behavior will continue.

Next time, Ginger accidentally tips over a nearby plant stand as she gets into the trash. Pots, plants and watering can come crashing down, sending her racing away in fright. This time trash tipping had a negative consequence, and Ginger is less apt to get into the trash again.

"Ginger, Come"

Ginger comes when you call and receives praise, a smile, a pat on the head and her dinner. The word *Come* resulted in a good association. She's apt to be interested in running up to you the next time she hears that word.

This time you call Ginger over to you because it's time to trim her nails. She comes but is not at all happy with the nail clipping. She may think twice before coming the next time you call her.

"Ginger, Bad!"

Those examples are pretty straightforward, but it can get complicated. Suppose Ginger is about to chase a cat into the street. You admonish, "Ginger, Bad!" Does she think she's bad because:

a. she was stepping into the street (but we do it at every corner);

b. she was chasing a cat (I shouldn't do that);

c. she was near a mailbox (I must now avoid them at all costs);

d. she saw a child (maybe children are bad and to be feared);

e. she didn't catch the cat (I'll be faster next time, promise); or

f. _____; you fill in the blank (or Ginger will).

You may gain insight into the training process by looking at life from a different point of view—your dog's. As with Ginger's cat-chasing experience, there are times when an aspect of a learned behavior is irrelevant to the owner but key to the dog. You may be training one thing, but your dog learns something entirely different—and entirely unexpected.

THE DOG'S POINT OF VIEW

Even experienced dog trainers sometimes have difficulty seeing things from a dog's point of view. Eight-week-old Lacey, an English Cocker Spaniel, arrived at our house late in October. As part of our standard house-training for all of our dogs, we began to teach Lacey to sit by the door and wait for someone to let her out into the far end of the backyard to the designated toilet area, "Over there." All seemed to be going well except on cold, snowy days. On those days Lacey would sit to be let out as usual, but instead of walking off the deck into the yard to the toilet area, she would potty right on the deck. The family began to call it the Poop Deck.

What could be going wrong? This was a tried and true method. All of our other dogs successfully learned this behavior. "You should have gotten a *real* dog," said a not-too-helpful family friend, referring to the fact that we both owned German Shepherds. "No, I wanted something small and sporting" I replied. "Then you should have gotten a Corvette," he retorted.

"She's being wimpy," my son volunteered. "She's not as smart as my Golden, Mom," my daughter offered. "She's cold," my husband suggested. "You shouldn't take so much fur off when you groom her; better buy her a coat."

Pride and love of this puppy (she's much cuddlier than a sports car) urged me to get to the bottom of the problem. She was OK unless it was really snowy. A good clue, but how could I use that information to solve the problem?

With careful observation and documentation, the mystery was solved. When it was snowy, the deck was completely covered with snow, just like the backyard. When it warmed up, the snow either melted, or we got out there and swept it off the deck. During the backyard training sessions, Lacey was invariably rewarded for toileting in the snow since there was snow everywhere. Each time it snowed again and covered the deck, in her mind the deck was then fair game. If there was no snow on the deck, she would step down into the yard like a good girl— in search of snow. Lacey had learned to potty on snow, not "over there"—as I *thought* I was teaching her.

When we finally caught on, the jokes were flying about the spring thaw! As the snow started to disappear, Lacey went farther and farther into the shady parts of the yard to find some snow. Spring came and she figured out that grass was OK too.

THE POOP DECK

Dogs are contextual learners. Although we never know for sure the exact association a dog is making in training, the techniques in this book will increase the odds that you will communicate successfully with your dog.

Chapter 2

The Second Foundation Stone: Understanding Your Dog

Over the years I've lost count of the number of people who have told me they had the best dog in the world. I often wondered how that could be, since without a shadow of a doubt *I* had the best dog in the world. I guess if you don't live with the best dog in the world you either (a) don't deserve your dog or (b) should do some training.

A Mentally and Physically Fit Dog

Harvey was a good dog. Tolerant of strangers, he rarely even barked when the doorbell rang. He was especially fond of children and enjoyed an invitation to play when he met another dog on walks. Recently, while he was sniffing along on a walk in the park with his owner, a dog came bouncing up to play and Harvey snapped at her. A similar incident occurred a week later when one of the children's friends got up from watching television to get a drink. On the way back out of the kitchen, the child casually reached down to pat Harvey, and he growled. Should the family punish him?

A trip to the veterinarian revealed that Harvey had cataracts. Imagine driving a car through severe fog on a dark night. Approaching cars, telephone poles—they seem to jump out of nowhere. Now that the owners know the problem, they can take special measures to keep Harvey out of situations where he might be startled.

Veterinary care is a very basic management issue. It's an often overlooked first course of action for training and behavior programs. A significant change in behavior is one of the first signs of an illness. For example, you're coming down with the flu and the noise of children playing bothers you. This is out of character for you. "Unpredictably, and for no reason at all," you become aggressive with the children. . . .

Orthopedic disorders, parasite infestation, hormonal imbalances, neurological problems, dietary deficiencies and other maladies can greatly affect behavior. In addition, pharmaceutical intervention is a possible adjunct therapy for a number of behavior problems. If you plan to visit your veterinarian with a specific behavior concern, tell the receptionist so the doctor will be prepared to ask the appropriate questions.

Ask your veterinarian about spaying your female (ovariohysterectomy) or neutering your male (castration). A definite aid in pet population control, there are health and behavioral benefits as well. Neutering could well extend your dog's life span. Diseases of the reproductive organs are eliminated, and mounting, marking, roaming and interdog aggression are greatly reduced, especially in male dogs. One of the biggest behavioral reasons to spay or neuter is the reduction in stress, which is at the root of many behavior problems.

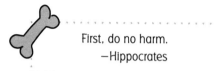

First, do no harm.
—Hippocrates

Make an appointment now. Take this book with you, and show your veterinarian the type of training you intend to do. Ask if there are any physical problems that need to be resolved before you launch your training program. Your vet is a valuable local resource who can refer you to people who specialize in canine behavior and training in your area.

Temperament and Breed-Specific Traits

Over the centuries, humans have selectively bred dogs for certain traits that were considered desirable at the time. These breed-specific characteristics can be quite strong and can also be obvious in mixed-breed dogs. Some of these natural behaviors, which we now find problematic due to our lifestyles, are simply the dog's attempt to satisfy instinctual demands. When assessing your dog's behavior, consider the nature vs. nurture question. You may train your dog to do one thing (nurture), but nature is whispering another. Go *with* the drives, not against them. We are the ones who domesticated dogs; let's help them fit comfortably into our society.

Historically, chasing and nipping was in the job description of many of our modern breeds. Running with children or similar situations may overexcite such dogs. Get a handle on these instincts by playing retrieve games, but play by your rules and maintain control of the game.

Dogs that were bred to live with the flock and guard against predators are apt to be aloof and self-confident. Their role in life is to work independently. Gaining the cooperation of working dogs with this background might take extra effort.

> Temperament is the interaction between a dog's genetic predisposition and the environment in which he or she lives.

Digging holes was required behavior for numerous breeds of dogs, including terriers. You may have more success in redirecting the digging behavior to a "legal" digging area, rather than trying to stop it altogether.

Running with wild abandon was an essential behavior for some hounds. Work on motivational recalls early on to keep these dogs safe and under control, and consider that perhaps some dogs can't be off leash in tempting situations. If your dog likes to run, make that a reward after a brief obedience exercise of your choosing if you have a safe, enclosed exercise area. The dog could well learn to get through, even enjoy, your lesson in anticipation of the run.

In any individual dog, we do not know whether nature will ultimately prevail over nurture or the other way around. Will a friendly, outgoing dog continue to be so in a neglectful family? Or will the dog become distrustful and hostile in that environment? Can a naturally fearful dog be socialized and trained to readily accept people? Finding the answers to questions like these is our challenge. To do so, we'll need to be able to understand and communicate with our dogs. Only then can we train and mold their natural responses into behaviors we both enjoy.

> Trainers only have questions; the dogs have the answers.

Body Language

Canine body language is complex—too complex for simple explanations. The displays are many and varied, and some of the signals are subtle and ambiguous. But we can make a few basic generalizations.

Baseline Posture

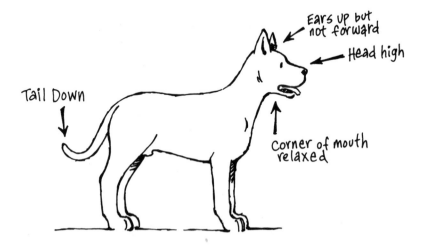

Ears up but not forward

Head high

Tail Down

Corner of mouth relaxed

Here's a middle-of-the-road type of dog. Compare this baseline position to the following drawings to see how postures and expressions change, depending on the mind-set of the dog.

Submissive Posture

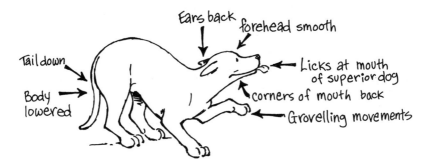

This dog is demonstrating subordinance. His body is low and his tail is tucked. His facial expressions indicate submissiveness by the pulled back ears, the averted eyes and the downward-drawn corners of his mouth. He is avoiding extended eye contact by turning away. He may make small groveling movements, flick his tongue or even dribble urine. He's showing deference to his leader with these appeasement gestures. Some of these subordinate displays border on, and at times overlap with, displays of anxiety. While respect for his leader is important, an overly submissive dog could pose a training problem. Positive methods are certainly in order and can be very effective in training this dog.

Offensive Posture

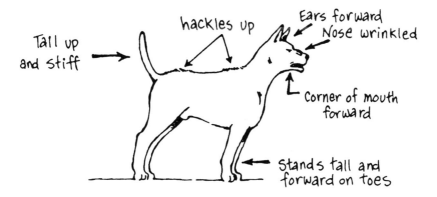

Here is a dog displaying offensive body language. An offensive dog is trying to gain control of an important resource. The body postures of an offensive dog make the animal appear larger. The attitude is fearless, confident, assertive and bold. Like an offensive fullback on a football team, this dog is out to score. Think of a Zulu warrior. The warrior carries both shield and spear. If he uses the spear, he is being offensive—the unabashed challenger ready to attack others. He's the one calling the shots, the one commanding the situation.

While an offensive dog can be trained to be a good companion, the average owner lacks the skill needed to manage an offensive dog. Fortunately, there are few truly offensive dogs. If you feel your dog is offensive, ask your veterinarian for a referral to a local behavior consultant, or check the resources in the back of this book.

Defensive Posture

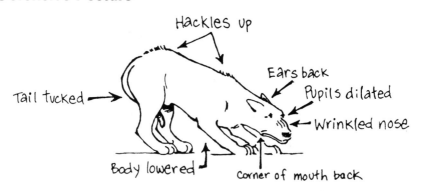

Next we have the body language of a defensive dog. The body postures of a defensive dog are in many ways the opposite of the offensive dog. They are low to the ground, as if the dog is trying to protect vulnerable parts of his body. A defensive dog is trying to protect himself or important resources from interlopers that invade the "critical distance"—the distance at which the dog no longer feels safe. If the intruder is chased out of the critical zone, the dog will often withdraw the threat.

Although the actions of a defensive dog might be misinterpreted as bold, those actions are based in fear. The dog may have learned from past experience that offensive language works to keep threats at bay. Beneath that bluster, the dog is actually hesitant, nervous and distrustful. Like a defensive lineman on a football team, the defensive dog is protecting his own interests by trying to keep the other team from scoring. This dog is not a warrior using a spear, but rather wields the shield to fend off the enemy and simply protect himself. Still, this dog may strike out when it seems that escape or defense is not enough to rebuff the aggressor.

More dogs fall into this category than the offensive category. Because it's difficult to predict what a defensive dog perceives as a threat, rehabilitation is beyond the scope of this book. Once again, ask for a local referral.

Other Signs

Tails also tell a tale. A wagging tail doesn't always mean a friendly dog, but simply indicates some type of excitement or arousal. These emotions can include happiness, anxiety, anger, hunger or romance. A dominant dog will hold its tail high, wagging in a small arc, while a lower tail carriage and a faster wag indicate a more subordinate animal. Tails are confusing, especially when you consider that some dogs have tails curled tightly over their backs and others have no tail at all. Read the rest of the body.

Bowing is another type of body language. Often a bow is the dog's way of soliciting play or appeasing another. The dog will lower her front end and wag her tail. Sometimes a bow is evidence of an inward state of confusion, of being ready to do something but not sure of exactly what.

IDENTIFYING STRESS

It was the first night of dog obedience class. Mrs. Edwards was looking forward to taking Murphy to class to teach Murphy once and for all not to pull on the leash. Class turned out to be a miracle cure because Murphy immediately learned not to pull on the leash. In fact, he wouldn't even walk.

It started before they even got into the classroom. Murphy balked at climbing the stairs to class and had to be carried up the steps. He had never seen anything so scary. There was only one step at Murphy's house, the front door step. In class Murphy began to shake and pant. He hid behind his owner's folding chair during the orientation. He was yawning continually, even though he wasn't tired. Murphy was under pressure. He was anxiety ridden. In common terms, he was stressed.

Perhaps it was the slippery floors in the hallway to class. His house was fully carpeted. Maybe it was the Great Dane next to him. He liked dogs but had never seen a 125-pound black dog at such close range. Could it be Mrs. Edwards fidgeting with the leash and saying, "It's OK, it's OK"? Murphy was wondering why she was so nervous. Her attempt at calming him made Murphy even more tense.

What can we do for Murphy? Read on about stress, and then we'll get back to Murphy later.

There's good stress and bad stress. Stress in manageable doses has a positive effect on individuals. It helps us perform to our potential. Deadline coming? Productivity goes up. To a point. Too much stress can produce distress, and too much distress can produce disease. Severe cases of stress need to be evaluated quickly, before the problem escalates into an illness or before the situation endangers others if the dog does something aggressive out of frustration.

Stress is also linked with numerous behavior and training problems, and that's what we will focus on here. Causes of this type of stress in dogs are subjective and require careful observation. The dog will tell you most of what you need to know, but identifying the signs of stress can be tricky. The signs are ambiguous. It's important to look for clusters of indications, rather than just one.

For years doggy experts have talked about the three F's exhibited by fearful and stressed dogs:

- **Freeze**—Playing statue. A dog that freezes, frequently in a "small" or subordinate position, is likely afraid and stressed.
- **Flight**—Some dogs choose retreat, running and hiding from the cause of the worry.
- **Fight**—Yet other dogs resort to aggression—growling, lunging, snapping and biting—when their stress level is pushed beyond their ability to cope.

By the time we see one of the three F's, the dog is often already out of control. We need to watch for the precursors to the three F's, the more subtle signs that a dog is worried.

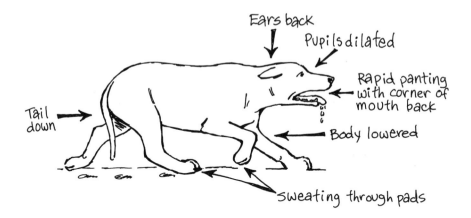

Ears back
Pupils dilated
Rapid panting with corner of mouth back
Tail down
Body lowered
Sweating through pads

Vocalization. Repetitious barking without an apparent reason may be a compulsive behavior caused by stress. This may be the dog's way of masking or ignoring the unpleasant situation.

Change in toilet habits. Diarrhea or a sudden lapse in house-training is often one of many subtle signs of a dog under stress.

Panting. A dog that pants when it's not hot may be stressed. Panting also is an indicator of physical problems. Or maybe the dog just went for a run.

Sweaty paws. Why are there wet paw prints on the tile floor? It's not wet outside. Consider stress. Dogs perspire through their paw pads.

Tense body. Rigidness is an indication of a stressed dog. Sometimes you have to actually touch the dog to feel the tension. At other times you can see tension just by the way the dog holds its body or moves. Also, look for a clenched mouth and jaws.

Shedding and dandruff. Excessive hair on the veterinary examining table or the training hall floor may be an indication of stress or other physical problems. Regardless of when the dog was last brushed, anxiety and the associated tensing of the body can help work loose hair out in a hurry.

Eyes. If your dog is wide-eyed but it's not particularly dark out, the dilated pupils could be a sign of stress. The eyes of some very frightened dogs will show more white than normal.

Drooling. If drooling cannot be related to anticipation of food, sexual arousal or an upset stomach, look for a hidden cause—stress.

Trembling. Again, we must look for clusters of signs, but shaking can be one indication of stress. A dog might tremble from the cold, but if it's not cold out a different stressor could be at work.

Talk to your veterinarian. Some of these signs can be indications of serious physical problems.

Calming Signals

Dogs may react to stress by engaging in what may seem on the surface to be irrelevant actions. Dog experts have a variety of labels for the behaviors about to be described: subordinance displays, cut-off signals, appeasement gestures, displacement activities, rituals and drives. Some of these terms describe the same behavior; some of the meanings overlap; some are entirely different and are used incorrectly. For simplicity, let's set language aside and simply describe what we might see happening.

Many experts believe dogs use the following behaviors as a way to communicate "Don't bother me and I won't bother you." They can be thought of as the dogs' attempts to calm themselves.

Yawning. Yawning in humans often occurs at critical moments of worry or apprehension, rather than when we're tired or bored. Breathing deeply helps reduce stress in humans. Dogs also yawn when things are getting tense. Perhaps the deep inhalation and subsequent exhalation of a yawn acts in the same way for them as it does for us.

The term calming signal comes from Norwegian behavior expert Turid Rugaas. Turid's full-time occupation is rehabilitating fearful dogs

Stretching the Tongue. A quick little flick of the dog's tongue often goes unnoticed because it is clouded by more obvious signals. It's another way for a dog to convey the same calming message. Both yawning and tongue flicking will often appear in photographs, because posing for a photo session can be stressful.

Scratching. A dog that scratches itself even though it doesn't have itchy skin may be diffusing stress. This is often seen in situations where a little itch would be inconsequential, for instance in the face of a confrontation.

Turning Away. To avoid a head-to-head confrontation, dogs will turn their eyes, their head or their entire body away from the problem, as if to say, "I'm not worried about you, not even enough to look at you." This behavior may also show subordinance—the opposite of confrontational face-to-face, eye-to-eye contact.

Shaking Off. Similar to shaking off after a swim, this motion is often seen after a dog is released from a tense situation. It's a way to say, "Phew! Glad that's over. Now I can relax." Some dogs, when excited, raise the hair on their backs a little. Perhaps the dog is getting its coat back in order, or perhaps it's trying to get back to normal after tensing up the skin and muscles. Encourage a nervous dog to shake by ruffling its coat backwards.

Sniffing. Dogs use their noses to explore their environment, but excessive sniffing can be a calming signal. This dog is trying to show indifference about what's going on.

Blinking. When two dogs approach, they are both aware and interested in each other. Why, then, do we see dogs looking away or exaggerating a blink? It is not disinterest or distraction, but a calming signal. You can gain the confidence of a worried dog more quickly by avoiding direct eye contact and by turning your side to the dog.

Comic relief. We do it too! We giggle or act silly when we're most nervous or embarrassed. Dogs may act silly by leaping into the air for no apparent reason, doing little spins or rolling vigorously on their backs.

What You Can Do About Stress

Just as we can use body postures such as standing sideways to give a dog confidence, we can also use more subtle calming signals. Rather than intensifying a situation by focusing on it and trying to reassure the dog, demonstrate how relaxed you are and that all is well by breathing deeply and relaxing your body. If the dog looks at you, blink your eyes slowly, yawn and turn away, and avoid eye contact.

An ounce of prevention is worth a pound of cure. That's why it's a good idea to select a dog with a personality that's compatible with your lifestyle. When looking at dogs, find a middle-of-the-road type that is not too pushy and has an energy level similar to yours. The dog that is hanging back may not be the best choice for you. Fearful and shy dogs need a lot of extra attention and training to live a problem-free life. Can you handle the one that's bouncing around, totally entertaining you and making you laugh? That one might turn out to be a Lamborghini, when perhaps a Chevy would be a better match for you.

The Touch That Teaches

Massage can work wonders for reducing stress in humans. When a dog is stressed, the body muscles become tense. This tension adds to the original anxiety. Many touches have been developed to relieve this tension. Here's an introduction to a couple of touches I have found helpful.

A type of touch therapy known as TTouch (pronounced *tee-touch*), developed by Linda Tellington-Jones, can help calm unfocused, fearful or easily excitable dogs. The basic TTouch involves simple circular movements. The three middle fingertips are placed on the dog's skin and moved clockwise to make a one and a quarter circle. The fingers don't move over the surface of the skin, they gently push the skin around in a circle. Envision a clock: The fingers start at six o'clock and make a full circle using just enough pressure to move the skin over the underlying muscle. When the fingers get back to six they move upward to nine o'clock and stop. These circles are done randomly about the body for three to five minutes.

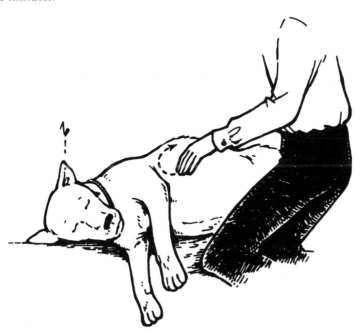

Throughout the ear there are nerve endings that relate to the entire body. Ears can be stroked to reduce stress by gently grasping the base of the ear between your thumb and first finger, close to the dog's head. With a soft, steady pull, ever so gently, slowly pull your fingers to the outer edge of the ear. This is repeated in overlapping sections until the entire ear has felt the touch.

If you'd like to learn more about this type of therapy, check the resources in the back of this book.

Specific Stress Tools

Upcoming chapters will be outlining behavior modification techniques. If you are interested in reducing you dog's stress, pay particular attention to the following tools described in Chapter 7.

Eliminate the Cause. Although it's not always possible, the simplest solution to stress is to remove the cause. As an example, busy families with small children don't always realize that their dog may need some time alone and that even tolerant dogs can run out of patience. Remove the cause by designating an area where the dog can retreat and where children are not allowed.

Improve the Association. Use a strong, pleasant association in the face of something stressful. If the dog dislikes taking her pill, turn it into a rare delicacy. Cat food is usually a no-no, as is eating from people utensils. Keep a small resealable can of cat food in the refrigerator. Put the pill on a spoon, dip it in and cover it with the smelly, fishy delight. Your dog will think she's really getting away with something.

Systematic Desensitization. It's possible to systematically desensitize a dog to a particular problem. If a dog is afraid of riding in a car, deal with it step-by-step:

- Walk the dog around your driveway.
- Walk the dog around the car when it is not running (exhaust, vibration or sound may be a meaningful part of the problem).
- Place the dog on the seat and allow him to jump out.
- Open doors on both sides and call the dog through the car.
- Do the above with the engine running, being careful not to get close to the exhaust.

As a tool, Systematic Desensitization works best in combination with other tools—Improving the Association, for instance. Pair the desensitization steps with a pleasant state of affairs. Some ideas:

- Play ball in the driveway.
- Circle the car while giving your dog tidbits.
- Place the dog's favorite toy and rug on the seat of the car.
- Feed dinner in the car.
- Sit in the car (in the driveway), read a book and pet the dog.
- Turn on the engine and do some positive things in and around the car, but be careful of carbon monoxide.
- Your first drives should be short—only a few minutes—and should include a good place to stop off for fun, like a park.

Back to Murphy

Murphy had a tough first night at obedience class. Could Mrs. Edwards have taken Murphy to the training site ahead of time, when there is no pressure to pay attention and learn? Perhaps he lacked socialization with other people, dogs and indoor locations. Could she have brought a familiar rug from home for him to lie on? Was he used to and happy riding in the car?

Mrs. Edwards was looking forward to taking Murphy to class to teach him once and for all not to pull on the leash. Could some of the preliminary training taken place in the comfort of his own home? Progressive trainers are giving their students homework head start programs, which increase success and decrease stress in the classroom. It's hard to concentrate and learn in stressful situations. There are some easy exercises described in Chapter 6 that could help Murphy settle into the classroom experience with less anxiety and fewer problems.

Murphy balked at climbing the stairs to class and had to be carried up. There was only one step at Murphy's house: the front door step. Could his fear of the stairs have been anticipated? Perhaps Murphy could have been taken to a building with stairs ahead of time. Mrs. Edwards could carry him to the last step, put him on it and allow him to walk off the staircase, then progress to the next-to-last step. She could simply walk to the top of the stairs and, as a matter of fact, invite him to join her. It's helpful to find a short, less daunting flight of only three or four steps and to start on carpeted stairs, which are easier to negotiate. And most dogs prefer stairs that you cannot see through; that is, the back of the stairs should have solid risers.

In class, Murphy began to shake and pant. He hid behind Mrs. Edwards' folding chair during the orientation. Be sure the class you sign up for has knowledgeable instructors. Instructors who have done their homework will have strategies for dealing with first-night jitters. They know how important it is to gain the dog's confidence so he wants to come out of hiding, rather than forcing him to participate.

Perhaps Murphy's problem was with the slippery floors in the hallway to class. His house was fully carpeted. Mrs. Edwards could get Murphy used to slippery surfaces by putting a plastic tarp down in her home and putting his food bowl in the middle. In class the instructor could take the leash and Mrs. Edwards could go sit down and invite Murphy to join her. Murphy will probably overcome his fear to get back to security, his owner. Fortunately, Murphy was a small dog. He could be carried just a few feet into the slippery area and placed on the floor, giving the leash to a helper. Mrs. Edwards might be a few feet away, near the exit door, rattling her keys. But be sure Murphy *does* get to leave, if only for a few minutes, or he will lose trust in his owner.

Maybe it was the Great Dane next to Murphy. He liked dogs, but had never seen such a big dog up close before. The instructor might place Murphy and Mrs. Edwards near dogs that are settled in nature and less threatening in appearance. Be sure Murphy has a place in the room with no traffic behind him. Not in a corner; there should be space for him to retreat. The idea is to provide a place where the fewest people and dogs will have to get close. He'll feel more secure this way. The instructor should also help the owners prevent eye contact between dogs.

Could it be Mrs. Edwards fidgeting with the leash and saying, "It's OK, it's OK"? Murphy was wondering why she was so nervous. Her attempt at calming him made Murphy even more tense. Hopefully, the instructor will give Mrs. Edwards positive things to do such as circling the chair now and then to get Murphy up, breathing, moving those tense muscles and thinking of her, rather than the stressful surroundings. Otherwise, Mrs. Edwards should ignore Murphy for the most part and let him sort it out. If he looks up at her in a worried manner, she should put a ho-hum look on her face, turn away, yawn and narrow her eyes as if she's not a bit worried at all.

As Murphy begins to relax, Mrs. Edwards may be able to interest him in something other than what's going on around him. Some instructors issue "pacifiers" for this purpose. One of my favorites is a nylon chew bone in the shape of a brontosaurus. Because the tail curls into a loop, I am able to slip a length of ski rope through the tail and knot it so it can't pull back through. Now we have a chew toy on a leash. The other end of the dinosaur's leash can be tied to the leg of the chair the owner is sitting on or simply held to prevent the toy from sliding away. It can be made more interesting by putting a bit of peanut butter on it. The instructor could try this, and when Murphy appears calm, reward the behavior by offering Murphy another dab of peanut butter for his dinosaur. This ensures Murphy will like the instructor, too!

Throughout it all, Mrs. Edwards should think of something peaceful: her favorite lounge chair, her last vacation or her favorite relaxation CD. We want Murphy to pick up on her calmness. Better yet, the instructor should be playing relaxing music in the background.

A dog that is not confident in his ability to handle an unusual situation is likely to experience stress. Showing an unsure dog that you are a capable leader will lessen the burden for your dog, who now feels safe deferring to the leader. The ALPHAbetize Yourself program in Chapter 4 is an appropriate leadership program.

I'll bet you can think of several more ideas to help Murphy (and Mrs. Edwards) relax. One of the goals of this book is to help *you* be more creative at coming up with your own ideas.

The Third Foundation Stone: Building an Appropriate Environment for Your Dog

Rosie is seven months old. She's a house dog. When she was a pup she went for lots of walks, but not so much anymore now that she's big. She has a habit of jumping on people and pulling the leash, so no one wants to walk her, which just leaves her with even more energy to burn. While the family is gone from 7 A.M. to 6 P.M. each working day, she stays indoors. Rosie has pulled up some of the carpeting, has chewed the legs of some furniture, leaves nose smears on the front win-

dow and the neighbors say Rosie barks a lot. On weekends the family locks Rosie out into their spacious fenced yard because they feel she needs the exercise, but Rosie just stands around at the door. Rosie needs a few adjustments to her environment!

ENRICHING YOUR DOG'S ENVIRONMENT

In the last decade there's been a new awareness of the human-animal bond and how association with dogs can enrich our lives. It's a two-way street! Even though time is often short, with a little creativity we can find ways to help our dogs lead fuller lives. The home-alone issue is a major factor in the problems people have with their dogs. Following are a few toys, games and activities that might help Rosie stay busy and happy. Some of these suggestions will be appropriate for your lifestyle. But be creative; use the examples as an inspiration to think of more ways to enrich your dog's life.

Making the Most of Your Time Together

Tourist! Take your dog for a ride when driving around town on short errands such as going to the post office or taking the children to school. Not much physical activity, but a change of scenery! It would only take a couple of minutes more to stop off at an interesting place on the way home for a brief walk or a training session.

When your dog goes for a ride, use a crate, wagon guard or doggy seat belt.

If you plan to go for a walk, keep your dog on leash and bring your plastic bag!

Don't leave your dog tied in front of a shop; all sorts of things could happen while you're gone.

Hide and Seek. A good indoor game or one for a fenced yard. Have a helper hold Rosie by the collar or leash. Better yet, teach her to stay and make her wait by herself. Make a big deal of leaving: "Good-bye Rosie, see ya later," while you go out of sight to hide behind a chair, under the bed or in an open closet. Rosie is then released to find you. If she gets off the track, just call her name.

This is a positive game that builds the bond between you and your dog. You might want to up the ante by taking Rosie's dinner bowl with you, or perhaps the joyful reunion can end with a game of fetch. If you have two dogs, one can hide with the owner while the other seeks.

BYOD Barbecue. Invite some friends over for a Bring Your Own Dog backyard cookout. Make it a fun evening by inviting people with dogs that you know play well together. On a hot day you might fill a child's plastic wading pool with some water and allow the dogs to play with floating toys or just jump and splash about. My dog enjoys "going fishing": Jam a small hunk of cheese in a hollow chew toy and throw it into the pool. Kong™ dog toys and commercially prepared toy bones are good for this. There may be more than one species of "fish" in the pool. My dog's favorite is peanut butter.

If the dogs become too worked up or rowdy, have a time out and ask the dogs to lie at their owners' feet for ten minutes.

Game Night. If it's too cold for a barbecue, invite a couple of friends with nice dogs over for an evening of indoor games. Consider the variables of space, the personalities of the dogs (and humans!) and the dogs' varying skill and energy levels. Be creative and think up interesting events: How about an international theme? Or a seasonal theme? Adapt people games to become dog games: Instead of human charades, the dogs can do impersonations. Instead of the same old human board games, try a new board game for dogs. There are games that practice basic obedience and games just for a good time. The best games are played for fun, not for competition. If you need some help, there are ideas in Appendix B.

Good Toy–Bad Toy. A structured way
to remind you to play with your dog,
this game also has an important message that carries over when your dog
is home alone. Have three appropriate dog toys spread out on the floor
along with an illegal object—like your
shoe. If Rosie investigates a dog toy,
mark her good choice with an enthu-

siastic "Yes!" and tell her how great she is and immediately have a play session
with Rosie and that toy. If she investigates an illegal object, ignore her. If she
persists in grabbing the wrong items, without emotion, pick up all the toys and
leave the room.

You can make the message clearer by making the good toys very good by putting
a tiny smear of cheese or butter on them. You can make the bad toys very bad by
spraying them with a taste deterrent, which can be found in most pet supply
shops.

Foraging. Foraging 101: Dogs were designed to hunt for their food. Working
for dinner is still good occupational therapy. A family member can hold Rosie
on her leash while you take her food bowl away and hide it. Come back and tell
Rosie to "Go find." Once Rosie learns to sit and stay, you can combine this
game with obedience practice.

Foraging 102: If Rosie eats dry kibble, occasionally feed her dinner by tossing
part of her meal onto your fenced lawn or patio. Now Rosie can have the fun of
hunting for her meal bit by bit. Use discretion. Lots of kibble, a big drink of
water and exercise can cause serious tummy problems for your dog. Troubleshoot all of your ideas—for instance, if you use pesticides or fertilizer in your
yard, keep Rosie indoors to forage.

Tug of War. Tugging games are a great way to exercise a dog, *if* the human
involved is smart enough to win the game. I don't recommend it for children.
The big problem is with the Give, not the Take. Some dogs don't want to give.

Teach your dog the rules before you play. Start by sitting down calmly with a
low-ranking, somewhat boring tug toy and a pocket of goodies. Put the toy in
the dog's mouth as you say "Take," then remove it as you say "Give" and pop in
a treat in its place. Work on this a few days before you start tugging.

If, while you are playing, the dog becomes overly stimulated or won't Give when
asked, stop playing, plant your feet, turn your head, put your hands and the

object close to your body and wait. The dog will eventually give up because it's not much fun. Sit down and do some calm Take, Give and treat sequences and play again. If you don't play again, the dog may just try harder to retain possession of the toy next time because she will have learned that Give means the game is over. If your dog is the type that might mouth your hand before giving in, apply a little bitter taste deterrent to your hands before you play.

Fetch the Ball. Retrieving a ball on a rope is fun if the dog brings it back and gives the ball up nicely. The rope allows you to use the same technique as tug of war to control the Give. But somewhere along the line some dogs seem to have lost their natural interest in chasing, grabbing and retrieving. There are plenty of games that don't involve retrieves, but if you want to teach fetch, start by tossing the ball down a hallway with all the doors closed to cut down on the distractions. As the dog chases it, quietly follow to give help if needed. Back up down the hall a bit, make a fuss over the dog, take the ball and it throw again. Quit while the dog is still having fun, exchange the ball for a tidbit of food if you're feeling generous and put the ball away. Or stand in the middle with two equally valued fetch toys. As he comes in with one, show him another and throw the second one in exchange for the first.

Beggar! This is a game for dogs that enjoy food and know how to retrieve. Once your dog understands the game, it can be played while you're busy with other chores. Find a toy that's soft but heavy enough to be thrown accurately. I've found Houston Chews™, a rope with a soft rubber ball in the middle, great for this game. Divide some of your dog's food into several portions. Add a special treat or two, something your dog really likes. (Remember to deduct the food for this game from your dog's daily allowance.) The basic game is to toss the toy and, when it's retrieved, exchange it for a portion of food.

Here are some variations on the theme: Put your dog on a Sit-Stay, throw the toy, varying the length of the Stay each time. Increase the difficulty by throwing the toy when the dog's not looking. Pick some challenging retrieves like up on a bed, behind a chair, out into your fenced yard! More than one dog? One can practice Down-Stay while the other plays, then switch. With two or more dogs you can stagger the starts after a brief Stay; throw each dog's toy in a different direction. I'll bet you are already thinking of your own variations.

If your dog understands scent discrimination, plant several decoy toys around the house, along with your ball and rope. Pay only for the delivery of the right toy. When the dog figures out the game and is good at it, randomize the reward: Sometimes you reward with the food treat, sometimes a pat on the head, sometimes a smile, back to the food treat, sometimes no reward at all. The pay schedule should never be predictable. When the food is gone, ceremoniously put the toy away, signaling the end of the game.

Set Your Alarm. And get up 15 minutes early to go for an extra walk or to prolong your morning walk. Instead of hitting the snooze button, hit the floor—with both feet and get going. If it's awful outside, spend that time playing with or training your dog inside. If your dog suffers home-alone anxiety, get up early enough so that you can completely ignore your dog for at least 20 minutes before you leave, lessening the impact of your departure.

Home Alone Activities

Latchkey Dogs! Too many of them spend their time in the backyard or in the house with not much at all to do. Unlike Ol' Shep, most dogs no longer get the opportunity to tag along with their owners day in and day out as they earn their living. Our urbanized society more often commutes to a workplace far from home. No more walking out to work in the field or going down to the barn for chores. People are just not as much fun as they used to be. Dogs invent hobbies such as recreational hole digging. Some pass the time by barking at pedestrians to keep them moving on through the neighborhood—it works!

Dog Door. Is there a reason your dog is not allowed indoors while you're gone? Most dogs prefer to be indoors, whether the people are there or not. The reason some dogs spend their days outdoors, falling into barking and digging habits, is because they were never successfully house-trained. Is it something a little training could overcome? If you have a secure, fenced yard (dig proof, jump proof, chew proof, squeeze proof), invest in a dog door to give your dog a choice of location and a bit more freedom and territory. Install a dog door so that instead of wondering what's happening inside or outside, the dog can check it out himself. These doors are reasonably priced, weather tight and easy to install.

Worried about the dog tracking in dirt? A strategically placed carpet runner can blot up most of it on the way in. By the way, don't trust your children or the meter reader to close the gate. The only safe gate is one that's locked or nailed shut!

Don't worry if you can't afford to fence your yard; most dogs just pick a couple of favorite spots to hang out anyway. Attach a chain-link run and dog door to a convenient room of your home and your dog will have a nice little fresh-air patio from which to view the world.

Dog Window. How about a dog window? If your dog is outdoors, a chain-link panel in a solid fence might be entertaining. Sort of like live television. Is the window idea appropriate for your dog? Will this create a barking problem at your house?

Dog Perch. Take a tip from Snoopy, but your dog won't have to balance on the top of the doghouse roof. A sturdy tip-proof, slip-proof platform in the middle of the yard, strategically placed so the dog can jump up and get a better view of the world over the fence, might provide entertainment. Just make sure it's not so close to the fence that your dog can use it as a springboard to escape.

Window Seat. A heavy, tip-proof chair by a window indoors might be fun. Troubleshoot the idea, though. Is your dog excitable enough to think about jumping out? Will he see more things to worry about or bark at?

Play Groups. When my children were preschoolers we belonged to a play group of two other families. We organized a schedule in which the moms would take turns hosting the other children in a morning play group once a week. We rarely had to worry about bored children on those days. They entertained each other all morning and slept all afternoon!

You might want to work out a similar arrangement with a friend who has a compatible dog. Compare weekly schedules and on days when someone is home to supervise, invite the other dog over.

Dog Walker. There have been professional dog walkers in business for years. Be sure to check references—lots of them! And it won't hurt to drive or walk around on a known route to see how the dogs are handled. How many dogs are walked together? Are they compatible or is one constantly pushed out of the way by another? A little bit of rank order is natural, but be sure all are having a good time.

If you're considering a friend or neighbor as a private walker, beware! This person might be a great friend, but objectively evaluate his or her ability to show your dog a good time and maintain control and security. Can your friend and your dog cope well with children, other dogs, or loud noises that might occur on the walk?

Doggy Day Care. Another great concept. Interview the proprietor and observe the day care in progress. Are large numbers of dogs turned loose together to play? Do you see obvious "underdogs" during the play session? Dog play requires a lot of give and take, but it only takes one bully for others to learn defensive, aggressive behaviors. Is there rest time for the dogs? Does there seem to be plenty of supervision? What is their policy on barking dogs? Do they correct this? How? How do they handle health issues? If you are purchasing a training option, what methods will be used in training?

Companionship Tape. You might want to record a tape of your family's voices and sounds of everyday household activities. The tape might keep your dog company but, more importantly, it will help mask outside noises that might cause anxiety. Some people use easy-listening music, and I have one student who taped her husband snoring. She reports that her dog prefers this to relaxing music.

Toys for the Dog

Experiment and find some safe, sturdy toys that reflect your dog's choice in games. Some dogs like chase games best, so a ball or flying disc might be appreciated. Other dogs prefer toys that allow them to tug, shake or chew—a rope, a nylon chew, a fleecy stuffed animal toy.

Some toys are cooperative toys to be played with together. Those are put away and brought out for specific interactive sessions. (More on that in Part II.) Other toys can be left out for the dog to enjoy at will. But only leave a couple of toys down at a time and rotate the toys every few days, so your dog will be less apt to lose interest in them.

The selection and use of doggy toys has become an art in itself. Allow your dog to try out all toys thoroughly before leaving them down when no one is home. If it appears the toy can break, or might be small enough to get lodged in the dog's mouth or cause frustration, get rid of it and try a different toy. Here are some ideas for you:

Nylon Chew Toys. Nylabone™ is a popular brand available in the shape of bones, rings and other interesting shapes. The most indestructible shapes are the Galileo and Hercules models, and I would use those for large dogs. Most of the medium and small dogs I know prefer the dinosaur shapes—brontosaurus to be exact! They're a little more difficult to find, but are well worth the search. The bumpy skin of the brontosaurus helps keep teeth and gums in good shape, but most important the curved neck and tail allow lots of nooks and crannies just begging for a dab of peanut butter, soft cheese or liverwurst. Just a touch of one of these tasty treats will make the dinobone irresistible and the legs of your furniture rather boring by comparison.

Hollow Rubber Toys. Your dog might enjoy a pine cone shaped rubber Kong™. It entertains by bouncing and rolling erratically when nudged or dropped. Buy one big enough that it won't get stuck inside your dog's mouth. Kongs can be stuffed with a portion of your dog's dinner, providing a pleasant pastime for an underemployed dog. Mixing in a couple of spoonfuls of canned food will keep dry kibble from falling out too quickly. So will a wad of bread. Be creative by layering jackpots, like a tiny piece of cheese or a bit of meat layered with kibble.

Make a hot weather pacifier by sealing off the small end of the Kong with peanut butter and filling it with water. Add a pinch of bullion powder and shake well. Stand it on end in a cup and freeze. Rinse the pupsicle with warm water before serving to get the frost off.

Planet Pet. This saucer-shaped rubber toy has three holes to grip doggy treats, giving you more mileage. These require more effort to get out less food.

Hollow Chew Bone. Commercially prepared hollow bones from a pet supply shop are a safer bet than bones from your butcher, which can splinter and cause health problems. These can also be made virtually irresistible by inserting just a little squeeze cheese (soft processed cheese in a tube).

You might consider providing several toys stuffed with goodies. I know dogs that spend the whole morning eating their entire breakfast out of their toys. The latest in toy stuffing ingredients is often a topic of conversation when dog trainers get together. Remember to keep the toys clean, especially in hot weather or where insects are prevalent. They do well on the top rack of the dishwasher.

Buster Cube. If your little predator isn't destined for backyard hunting expeditions, how about foraging indoors with the best thing since Pez: a food dispensing toy for dogs. Buster Cube™ mania is sweeping the dog world. Most trainers claim this is one of the best dog toys ever invented. It's a five-inch plastic block with a tubular maze through the middle. The cylinder holds more than a cup of kibble and can be twisted to adjust the flow of the food from slow to slower. Put one down and your dog will paw it, nose it, scoot it along the floor to get the kibble out. Depending on the degree of difficulty you program into your cube, the dog can be kept busy for a long, long time tracking food across the floor.

Dispenser Balls. Not as sophisticated as the cube, but it works along the same principles and gets the job done.

More than one dog? Dogs can get into arguments about ownership. Think this over before leaving your dogs home alone together with a prized possession. In some multiple dog families, highly regarded toys are for supervised play only.

Treasure Hunt. Prepare several hollow toys with a small yummy surprise in each. Before you leave home, hide the toys. Use some thought here; don't put toys where a dog might tip over furniture or get caught, frightened or injured. Build anticipation for the hunt by getting your dog to Sit-Stay while you hide the toys. Continue the Stay while you do all the things that predict you are about to leave: Put on your coat, find the car keys, get your briefcase. Be matter of fact when you release him and go to work. This downplays your departure and builds pleasant expectations for the treasure hunt.

Doggy Bags. A slightly different version of the treasure hunt is the doggy bag. Put a variety of toys and food tidbits in a brown paper bag. Hide it for your dog to find and raid. Some dogs extract these goodies politely, some will rip up the bag—maybe those guys need a doggy dishpan or other container that won't require cleanup when you get home.

A Chase Around Toy. I advocate fenced yards, but rarely do dogs take advantage of their good fortune by deliberately exercising themselves. This toy was invented by my friend who has several active Border Collies. Chase A Round™ is like tether ball for dogs. It provides an excuse to run, jump, grab, tug, shake— hours of fun while freeing up your throwing arm for other chores.

Spring Ball. Ball-oriented dogs can use some of their spare energy tugging a ball on a rope attached to a sturdy but supple tree branch. The spring action keeps the ball interesting because it plays back. If your dog doesn't like balls, you might try attaching a fleece dog toy to the rope. For safety's sake, check the toy and especially the branch for signs of weakness each time the dog is allowed to play.

Boomer Ball. These big, hard rubber balls are made especially for animals. My friend Kerrie field-tests new toys for me. If they get past her five American Stafford-shire Terriers, she takes the toy to work; Kerrie's a marine mammal trainer. If her sea lions don't break it, it's bound to be around your house for a while. Boomer Balls™ hold up to the sea lion test, and they come in a variety of sizes from big, bigger, bigger yet to biggest. Dogs either love Boomer Balls or totally ignore them. Too big to retrieve, dogs tend to enjoy pushing them around with their noses or have fun bumping them along with their front legs. You'll need to demonstrate it for your dog and play with him at first to get him hooked.

Rawhide. Rawhide chews and other natural animal by-products are a big hit with dogs, but dogs tend to get into trouble with them. Like any valuable resource, if there is more than one dog involved, competition could result. The rawhide can also get very limp and become caught in the dog's throat. And ambitious dogs can chew through rawhide with alarming speed, eating so much they get a belly ache.

A Word to Parents

When it comes to helping your dog and your child form a good relationship, the earlier the better. Here are some ideas for helping your child and your dog live happily ever after.

Infants

The key to infants and dogs getting along is supervision, supervision, supervision. Dogs and babies should not be left alone together. Most dogs get along just fine with infants, but why not do a little advance preparation for the new arrival to make sure the first meeting goes smoothly? Dogs that might cause concern are those who are spoiled, those who guard toys and food, those who are prey and chase oriented, dogs who are high in energy and out of control and those that try to get their own way, are touchy about their body or are grumpy in general.

All family dogs should be obedience trained. If a baby is expected, brush up on Sit, Down and Stay. Sit and Stay for greetings instead of jumping up on people should be well established. Being able to send the dog to a specific target area, such as a special rug, and have the dog remain there until released will be very helpful. Walking nicely on a leash is especially important now that you will have a baby buggy to control as well as a dog. Chapter 6 will help you with these concepts. Be sure your dog realizes that you are the leader and the decision maker by implementing as many of the ALPHAbetize Yourself concepts in Chapter 4 as are practical.

If anything in the dog's lifestyle will change, it should change before the baby comes home. For instance, if the dog is not allowed into the baby's room, now is the time to start boundary training the dog. Go into the room, tell the dog to Sit-Stay or send him to the target area. You might simply teach the dog not to cross the threshold into the room. Make staying outside the room very special and good. This is a time to give the dog a pacifying treat such as a chew toy or come out to him and pile on the attention.

Get the dog used to the baby before the baby comes home. Set up your crib and changing area ahead of time. Get a teddy bear or doll and place it in the crib. Baby So Real™ by ToyBiz is a 20-inch doll that cries, flails her arms and moves her eyes. A few times a day take a couple of seconds to go over to the doll. Sprinkle some powder or rub some lotion on the doll to get your dog used to these new activities and smells. Get a tape of an infant crying and play it while the dog eats or during other times your dog is happy. If the baby is born in a hospital, you can bring home a blanket that has the baby's scent on it. Wrap the doll in it and allow the dog to investigate this novel smell. Be happy and praise the dog.

It's a Boy! – Junior Meets Gretchen

It's been decided that Grandma will carry the baby into the house instead of Mom. That's because Gretchen may be so glad to see Mom she might forget her manners and jump up, causing ill feelings or endangering the child. Even if this doesn't happen, Mom might be nervous and Gretchen might be sensitive to that and worry, too. Mom will greet Gretchen, but not make such a fuss that the dog becomes overly excited. Allow Gretchen to sniff the baby all over, unless she's too excited and out of control.

Babies squeak and move like prey animals. These sights and sounds could initiate instinctual chase and grab reactions in Gretchen. Some dogs might simply want to investigate. Babies and dogs should not be left alone unattended.

In their first days together the baby should appear, in Gretchen's mind, to produce attention and happiness. You can accomplish this with little effort. For example, when Mom changes the baby, tidbits or balls can be tossed to Gretchen. An apron with big pockets will be handy! Or have a jar of treats or balls ready on the changing table. Mom should speak softly and lovingly to Gretchen while holding the baby. Allow Gretchen to be nearby for an occasional pat.

Toddlers

Beware! When your baby begins to crawl and walk, the situation changes and supervision is even more important. Never leave toddlers alone with a dog, even if the dog has been friendly and tolerant toward the child. A poke in the eye, a trip and fall onto the dog, or a loud scream into the dog's ear could produce an orienting reflex that might make the dog whip around and knock the baby over. Or worse, the child's actions might cause the dog to growl or snap, and in general have bad feelings about your child and others.

Gretchen should have an area of her own—a bed, a wire dog crate, an airline kennel, a carpet square—any easily identified space. It should be accessible to the dog, close to family activities but out of the traffic pattern. Take Gretchen to this area when things become chaotic. Another concept is to make a temporary waiting station (see page 41).

Give your dog a special treat when she's in her safety zone. Over time, she will learn to escape to this area when she wants to be left alone. Respect this. Junior and his visiting friends must be kept away from Gretchen's safety zone.

The Temporary Waiting Station

Use this as an aid while you are training your dog to stay in one place during distractions. Get a piece of plywood twice as long as your dog. Drill two holes in the middle, thread a leash through and secure it with just enough length to allow your dog to stand and sit without tension on the leash. Place this temporary waiting station flat on the floor within view of family activities. When your dog is attached to the station, she can see what's going on but her own weight on the plywood will prevent her from going anywhere.

You can make a deluxe model by putting self-adhesive carpet squares on the top surface, or a lightweight model for very small dogs by using pegboard instead of plywood. This type of restraint should be used only for a few minutes and only when someone is supervising. Part II of this book will show you how to teach your dog to Sit-Stay or Down-Stay on cue.

Kids and K-9s

The mistake most parents make is allowing children too much freedom to interact at will with the family dog. Some common but inappropriate actions are:

- Running
- Screaming
- Throwing themselves at the dog
- Too much hugging or hugging from behind
- Blowing at the dog's face
- Playing tug of war
- Teasing by pushing and shoving hands at the dog's face, until the dog reacts

Telling the children to stop is not enough. Help the kids play some of the good games listed earlier in this chapter.

What About Other Dogs?

Appropriate interactions with the family dog is a fine place to start, but now is a good time to teach children how to interact with dogs that belong to their friends and relatives and dogs they might encounter on the street. Junior should realize that most dogs like most children most of the time, but there are a few rules to follow.

Prevent-A-Bite

Many years ago, while working for the People-Pet Partnership at Washington State University's College of Veterinary Medicine, part of my job involved writing program materials about animals and children. The program I wrote on teaching children the proper way to interact with dogs, called Prevent-A-Bite, seemed to be very popular. Here are some important points from that program.

The people most frequently bitten by dogs are children. Usually the bite is not from a stray dog, but from the child's own dog or at least a known dog, such as Grandma's or the neighbor's. Children should be taught the following concepts:

Please Do leave dogs alone while they are eating or chewing a toy. If you reach down and pet the dog it might surprise and worry her. Do you always feel like sharing your candy bar?

Please Do leave the dog alone while she's sleeping. After playing hard all day, you like to relax awhile, too. The dog might be having a bad dream and think you are a part of it.

Please Do always ask permission from an adult before going up to anyone's dog, even if you know the dog. Ask Granny if it is Granny's dog. Ask the parents if you are visiting a friend. Dogs can't say "I don't want to play now," but grown-ups are pretty good at figuring out what dogs are thinking.

The side of the head or under the chin is the best place to pet a dog.

Please Do approach the dog from the side, never from the back or straight in front. Extend your hand and show the dog your knuckles. Be sure the dog sees you. Have you ever jumped when a friend touched you and you weren't looking? It's just not polite.

If the dog stretches forward to sniff or seems friendly, it's her way of saying, "How about a pat?"

If the dog pulls back and acts afraid or acts angry, don't pet the dog. It's her way of saying, "I don't feel like a pat."

You might be tempted to comfort her if she seems shy. Leave her alone; your attention may just worry her more.

Please Do knock on the neighbor's door and ask for help if your ball accidentally gets into their yard. If no one is home, ask your parents to help. Don't go into the dog's yard without permission. The dog might worry, just as you might if someone walked into your living room without an invitation.

Please Do keep walking past a dog in a parked car. Don't reach into a dog's car even if you know the dog. The dog may look like she wants to be patted, but she might worry that you may take something. Do you always feel like sharing your things with others?

If you encounter a dog that seems very angry, stand like a post. Posts don't run, they don't make any noise. They just stand still. Do the same as the post. The dog will likely sniff you and go away. If you look at the dog, move your hands, talk or run, the dog will take more interest in you and won't go away as soon.

A child's future attitude about dogs in general will be influenced by the family pet. Your dog's opinion of children in general will be affected by your child's actions. In a few short decades the children of today will be making and enforcing the laws regarding dogs. If for no other reason than that, do your best to be sure your child has a clear understanding of dogs and their role in society.

Chapter 4

The Fourth Foundation Stone: Providing Leadership

They loved Benji and Benji loved them back, but his family was starting to lose patience with him. Like some children, Benji was pushing the limits. He would grab laundry out of the hamper and race around the house inviting chase. He would get between the family members and the open refrigerator door, making it impossible to ignore him, much less reach the bottom shelf. On walks he'd charge out ahead to give an enthusiastic greeting to dogs and people alike. And it was impossible to read a book without him jumping on the couch and working his way between you and the book.

Some of this behavior is cute. It's endearing to know that your dog likes your attention, but when the family changes their adjectives from cute to pest, delinquent, incorrigible, it's time to teach Benji some manners.

ALPHAbetize Yourself is not a program for a dog that has already taken the lead and is challenging you with aggressive behavior. Such a dog may view the exercises in ALPHAbetize Yourself as insubordination on your part and may "punish" you accordingly. ALPHAbetizing is a way of life, not a rehab program. If you have a dominant aggressive dog, seek professional help in your area (see Appendix C for some resources).

How to **ALPHA**BETIZE **Y**OURSELF

Developing the proper relationship and lifestyle with your dog is paramount to successful training. By carefully structuring everyday interactions so they become subtle demonstrations of leadership, you can gain Benji's respect and cooperation in a way that is natural and fair to your dog; a way that encourages Benji to willingly take your lead in a lifetime relationship.

Like children, dogs need to be shown the way to get through life successfully. Our leadership takes away the undue stress of trial and error. It's my opinion that if we show our dogs that our decisions and guidance make a positive impact on their lives, they'll willingly allow us this responsibility. They'll be happier and more confident in your leadership when they realize they no longer have the responsibilities of the world placed squarely on them.

Dogs evolved as group-oriented creatures. Peaceful coexistence among group members increases the likelihood that all will survive in good shape for cooperative defense and obtaining food. Fighting within the group might injure individuals and put the whole pack at risk. United we stand, divided we fall. Animals that live in social groups benefit from a capable leader, called an alpha. We see variations on this social hierarchy theme all over: Clubs have presidents, wolf packs have alphas, towns have mayors, schools have principals.

Every dog needs leadership. ALPHAbetizing is a good tool for raising a well-adjusted puppy. The program will help a shy and fearful dog understand that the problems of the world are not on his shoulders alone; he can rely on his leader.

If a member of a group perceives a weakness in its leadership, a challenge may be in order. Survival of the fittest. If the current leader meets this challenge and proves worthy of leadership, all is well. If the leader doesn't pass this test, survival instincts dictate that another group member take over the job.

Benji should view you as top person on the totem pole, the chairman of the board, the chief executive officer. If not, opportunistic Benji might take advantage of a perceived weakness and put himself in charge. You might end up with a pushy, uncooperative dog that lacks respect for you. Commonly known as the alpha syndrome, it's at the root of many behavior problems.

The following analogy, made by William Campbell, will help make this clear. In this scenario, your dog is the passenger.

> Compare your dog's existence to a lifelong airplane trip—totally dependent on the pilot and crew for necessities, including one vital need: to feel **safe.** If the pilot appears incompetent and the crew isn't sure about what's going on, the passenger starts squirming with anxiety as the frustration of being unable to control the situation takes its toll. If the passenger tries to take control himself, he will be subdued physically or scolded roundly, which only heightens his frustration. This situation can be more frustrating if the crew can't speak the passenger's language fluently and communicates the wrong ideas.

A word of warning: In your enthusiasm for training, don't interpret every rambunctious, attention-seeking action as your dog's ploy for a takeover. Many dogs are simply rowdy, fun-loving, out-of-control dogs without a thought of commandeering your place as top dog. These dogs simply need their rowdy behaviors channeled to make life fun for both of you. The principles in the ALPHAbetize Yourself program apply to this goal, as well.

The following subtle but effective points will help you earn, rather than demand, your dog's respect. There are plenty of ideas here. Pick a couple that appeal to you. You might already be practicing some of these concepts. Good! You're ahead! Some may not be appropriate in your case. For instance, your veterinarian may have recommended free feeding for your dog instead of scheduled meals. No problem—just skip over that. Some of the program components may seem too difficult for you right now. If so, shuffle those points to the bottom of the list and get back to them later. If you are worried about your dog's reaction to any component in the program, just skip that one for now. There are plenty of exercises from which to choose. The idea is to start with the points that you feel will work—you know, the easy ones. Your pride and satisfaction in success will encourage you to try others.

Keep in mind that this program is to help prevent challenges, not rehabilitate a dog that is already challenging you. With that said, let's take a look at ALPHAbetizing Yourself.

Attention

A Follower Must Pay Attention to the Leader

Several times a day, help Benji make eye contact with you by tracing a line with your hand between his face and yours. You can make your hand more interesting by holding a small toy, one of his favorites. Squeakers, balls, Houston Chews and fleecy toys can all work well. As soon as that eye-to-eye lock is made, even for one second, say his name in a normal tone of voice and praise him as if he had just made a monumental step forward in training. He has! It's the beginning of a communication channel between you and your dog and an important step in future training. The word *Benji* should mean "pay attention, something great is going to happen." Be sure something great does happen. Throw the toy, play tug, jolly him up—whatever he likes, do it! That includes snapping on his lead and going for a walk.

Don't use his name in conjunction with punishment. Don't call his name to take him away from fun. Don't say, "Bad Benji!" For right now, we want him to love it when you call his name.

This is step one in getting him to come when he is called—an exercise that might save his life in an emergency. We are using the toy to produce eye contact; next we will shift to having the eye contact produce the toy. When Benji seems to understand that eye contact is in his best interest, you can build on your attention program. Try tempting him with the toy. Quickly hide it behind your back. He may try to run around and get it. Keep turning. Don't let him see the prize. At some point Benji will look up at you. Say his name and give him the toy.

The next step is to hold the toy at arm's length. He'll look at it, even try to get it. He can't until he makes eye contact with you and you say his name.

Earning Praise From the Leader

Dogs love attention and deserve to receive it. But alpha dogs often get carried away with their demands for attention. If you're in the easy chair reading the newspaper and Benji hits the paper with his nose or paw to let you know he's there, ignore him. Benji may follow up with another nudge or even a bark. He's commanding you to pay attention. Don't do it. You'll be obeying Benji's orders.

This doesn't mean you shouldn't give your dog lots of attention. Give him even more than before, but on your terms. Reverse the command-response sequence. Ask him to sit or lie down first. Where's the line between "I like you, how about a pat?" and "Pet me right here, right now and don't quit until I say so"? Use your own judgment. Look at the big picture. If your dog is a perfect angel but simply invites lots of petting . . . well, on the big scale of things, this is not high on the list of problems.

The Leader Controls Matters Concerning Food

Instead of Free Choice Feeding

Benji depends on you for food. Use this vital link to your best advantage and make it clear that the food is coming from you. Feed some of his food by hand, as described in other ALPHAbetizing exercises. The rest of his daily portion should be fed in scheduled meals rather than free choice. A full bowl on the floor at all times does not convey a distinct a leadership message; when you ceremoniously present your hungry dog with his meal, it does.

Some old practices die hard, such as feeding dogs once a day. It's the general consensus now that most adult dogs benefit from eating twice a day rather than having one big meal. Puppies need to eat even more frequently. These meals should follow a regular schedule. The benefits of scheduled meals include:

- You will know exactly when your dog is hungry—helpful if you are training with food rewards.

- What goes in on schedule comes out on schedule—house-training is so much easier with scheduled meals.

- You can avoid strenuous exercise right after a meal—it's possible for your dog to become seriously ill if he's too active when his stomach is full.

Present the meals within a range of time, say about an hour or so. The worse thing you can do is to get your dog into a habit of eating at *exactly* the same time each day. We wouldn't want to throw Benji into a panic on a day that you might be home late from work! Finished or not, pick the bowl up after 15 minutes.

Avoid Food Guarding

Get extra training mileage from dinner time. Instead of putting his meal down all at once, put Benji's empty food bowl on the floor within view. Walk over to the bowl and place a small portion of his dinner in it. Go about your business. When the food is gone, place a little more in the empty bowl. In addition to ALPHAbetizing yourself, you are conveying a subtle message of, "Don't ever worry about people getting near your bowl; people turn empty bowls into full bowls." An ounce of prevention is worth a pound of cure. Dogs seldom get into the habit of guarding their food when fed this way. It's also helpful if you vary the location of the bowls. To further up the odds in your favor, place two or three bowls down and rotate putting portions of food in them, waiting for one bowl to be empty before you place a portion in the other.

This is a program to prevent food guarding, not to cure it. If your dog has a food guarding problem, get help. Ask your veterinarian for a referral to someone who specializes in problem behavior.

Leaders Eat First

With only a few exceptions, the social structure of a pack dictates that the high-ranking animal eats first if he or she wants to. If one of your meals coincides with one of Benji's scheduled meals, make it a point to feed him after you have eaten. Prepare his bowl of food, but leave it on the counter while your family sits down to dinner. After a few minutes, you can get up and give Benji his bowl.

The dominant individual in a food hierarchy can get food from another, if so desired. No more whine and dine! For now, ignore begging behavior or prevent the dog from being nearby while you eat or prepare a meal. Down-Stay is good for this. Benji's going to get treats, only now it will be on your terms during training exercises, not on his terms.

Social Interactions

Leaders Control Interactions With Others

Most dogs come to life when the doorbell rings. If Benji is a door dasher, make sure he minds his manners. He simply can't take charge in this situation. Settle him before you go to the door. If he's not reliable on a Sit-Stay, ask another family member to control him with his leash or keep an extra leash tied to a heavy chair for this purpose. This is only a stopgap measure. In Part II you'll learn how to teach Sit and Stay, and how to direct Benji to a particular "station" at times like this.

Dogs, like wolves, are constantly running for higher office.

— Erich Klinghammer,
North American Wildlife Federation

When it's time for a walk, don't allow Benji to demonstrate to the whole neighborhood who's in charge at your house by pulling ahead to greet other people. This is not necessarily dominance—dogs just like to walk faster than people and get where they're going. Besides, the guy on the sidewalk might be good for a pat. But it's still a nuisance. In passing or pausing for a chat, make sure Benji stays at your side unless he's released for a turn to say hello.

Leaders Win Games

Have fun. Play with your dog. The laughter and exercise associated with cooperative play are good stress relievers for both of you. However, to teach Benji that you are the team captain, games should be played on your terms, not his. For example, a typical game of fetch with Benji calling the shots has him dropping a ball at your feet and backing up barking, inviting you to play. You throw the ball for a while and when Benji's tired, he takes the ball and runs off with it. Who is dictating the terms of this game of fetch? Benji has commanded you to play, decided when the game will be over and, in his opinion, won the game by keeping possession of the ball.

Play with your dog more, not less, but until Benji learns the rules you should be the one to initiate the game and end the game. Games of chase are a great outlet for dogs. Benji will understand who's in charge if you keep possession of the ball. A ball on a rope will be easier for you to control. They're readily available at pet supply shops, as are a fun variation, the Foxtail, which has a pretty nylon sleeve. Put the toy in your pocket

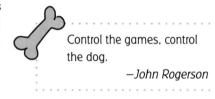

Control the games, control the dog.

—*John Rogerson*

or in a drawer when the game is over. Sound mean? Benji has plenty of his own toys. Once you have control of the games, it's not as important to hoard the ball.

Accept Handling by the Leader

Condition Benji to enjoy gentle handling and restraint. Conduct regular grooming sessions, telling him how great he is when he's cooperative. Even dogs with short coats can be gone over with a soft brush or a grooming glove. One or two very short, positive sessions are better than one long session. While you're at it, be alert for bumps, cuts, fleas and anything out of the ordinary.

Don't start with a battle. If your dog has a matted coat, splurge on a professional grooming job. Get a referral from your veterinarian for a groomer who uses gentle, dog-friendly techniques. Once your dog's coat is in order your own grooming sessions can be short, sweet and less stressful for you both.

If Benji has trouble keeping still, consider using peanut butter therapy. A tiny smear of peanut butter at nose level on a washable vertical surface, such as the refrigerator door, will distract, reward and control the dog's head for a few strokes of the brush. Once Benji's happy being handled, get him used to being up on a table or bench for grooming. It's easier on your back and it helps him accept being out of his territory and at ease in yours—or the vet's.

Muzzle Control Is a Natural Leadership Gesture

When dogs are playing among themselves, the one in the dominant role sometimes expresses his position by putting his mouth over the other dog's muzzle. We can talk to our dogs using their own language by mimicking some of these signals. Does Benji enjoy being stroked and petted? Finish by putting your hand over the top of his muzzle. Gently hold it there for a few seconds. Don't squeeze—this is not punishment, it's just a new ending to your routine petting and attention.

Some dogs may try to mouth your hand. If so, discontinue the muzzle control exercise until later in the ALPHAbetizing program when Benji's attitude adjustment is well under way. Another option is to apply a taste deterrent to your hands.

LEADERS CONTROL TERRITORY

Most of the world's wars have been fought over territory. But not everyone during those times really cared about the boundaries. Same with your dog. Territory may not be important to Benji; perhaps he places other valuable resources higher on his list. Benji may care more about food or toys, for instance, but teaching him to be mannerly and out of the way is still important.

The ALPHAbetize Yourself program is not entirely about rank reduction; it's about laying a foundation for training manners in general. Rank just happens to enter into it for a lot of dogs.

If you feel you need an edge on leadership, don't allow Benji to get into the habit of occupying strategic positions or passageways in your home. If Benji is lying down in a hallway or a doorway and you want to pass, ask him to move over or nudge him gently with your toe. Don't step over or around him, just say, "shoo, shoo, get out of way," and shuffle your feet in his direction or nudge him with your toe. If for no other reason than safety, he needs to keep out of people's way.

Provide him with a legal alternative for a resting place. Benji should be shown that there are places at home where he can relax undisturbed. You might be interested in providing him with a crate as his private den. Information is on page 144.

At your front door, car door or fence gate, Benji is apt to get excited and want to barge through ahead of you to see what's new on this part of his turf. This is a security risk and bad manners. Restrain him with the leash or a verbal command. Have him wait until you pass or until he is invited to go through.

Leaders Get the Best Resting Place

Owners of dominant dogs report that most challenges have occurred over possession of a resting place. The ALPHAbetize Yourself program is designed to help prevent these thoughts from entering your dog's mind. Companionship is one of the finest features of sharing your life with a dog. While life together is not a democracy, you can be a benevolent dictator. It's fine to have Benji in your bedroom, just not on the bed, until you are very sure he acknowledges you as leader. After a while, you can begin inviting Benji up for visits once in a while.

The same concept applies to chairs if you allow Benji on furniture. Periodically ask him to get off a chair. The first couple of times you can bribe him with a treat—a bribe makes getting down happen. Then you can graduate to rewarding him as soon as he gets down—getting down makes the reward happen.

If Benji is already giving you trouble over resting places, the ALPHAbetize Yourself program is not for you. Get some help from a pet problem professional (see the resources listed in Appendix C).

LEADERS ARE TEACHERS

Instead of concentrating on the negative, accentuate the positive! Train an acceptable behavior to take the place of the wrong behavior. Now you can reward instead of punish. Praise Benji for lying down for a pat rather than punishing him for jumping up on Junior. Reward him for sitting at the threshold instead of dashing out the door. One behavior competes with the other. Just be sure the one you want has the best reward! Chapter 5 will tell you how.

Supervise or Secure

Training and behavior modification takes a bit of time before dependable results can be achieved. Meanwhile, make sure your dog's antics do not get him into trouble. Keep in mind the terms *supervise* and *secure* as an immediate management strategy while you are training. *Supervise or secure* is a viable long-term solution to problems as well, particularly for behaviors that could harm the dog or those around him.

Supervise: "Puppy, I'll keep my eye on you the entire time you're upstairs on the new carpet until I'm sure you are house-trained."

Secure: "Puppy, I can't risk my new bedroom carpet. I'll have to restrict you to your crate in my bedroom at night, but we'll both wake up friends in the morning."

A Model for Leadership

The boss uses *I*.
The leader uses *we*.
The boss creates *fear*.
The leader inspires *trust*.
The boss *knows how*.
The leader *shows how*.
The boss relies on *authority* to get things done.
The leader relies on *cooperation*.
The boss provokes *resentment*.
The leader fires *enthusiasm*.

—Taken from *PPP Australia Handbook*

LEADERS ARE FAIR, KIND AND CONSISTENT

A long-term relationship based on trust will help keep communication channels open. This is the foundation upon which to build future training programs.

Part 11

Tools for Training Appropriate Behavior

Getting the Most Out of Reward-Based Training

You're hoping to stop bad behavior, but to do a good job you'll need to be ready to train a substitute, appropriate behavior. If you're clever about it, the good behavior will completely replace the problem behavior. Dogs already know most of the good behaviors we want to teach them. They know how to sit, lie down and be quiet. Our task is to gain control of these desirable behaviors, put them on cue. We need to communicate a few rules that govern these activities, and build them into the dog so that appropriate behavior is second nature.

Most of the training sequences in this book are based on positive reinforcement. We will set up situations where choices are to be made, we'll stack the deck in our favor and then reward the dog for making the right choice. This is a more natural, commonsense way to train a dog.

Training Rewards

We know that dogs repeat or increase behaviors that have been rewarded. We'll be using lots of rewards in the first stage of teaching. Over time, we'll decrease them until they're only given occasionally as a special thank you.

Encourage the whole family to participate in jotting down all of the things your dog considers a reward. Praise, petting, toys, going for a ride and playtime, all have been used as rewards in dog training. However, most of the exercises in this book are more effective if food is used as a reward.

Experiment and see what your dog likes best. A good reward will catch and maintain interest even with slight distractions. Be sure and view these rewards from your dog's point of view, not yours! You may be attracted to the pretty red plastic ball, when in fact your dog prefers the plain old gummy tennis ball.

Food

For the vast majority of dogs, the reward of choice is food. It's a primary reinforcer. To eat is to live. Dogs evolved from a long line of predators. Survival dictates that a predator be highly receptive to information associated with the acquisition of food. We can use some of these survival instincts to help us in training. Dogs no longer need to figure out how to catch their own dinner, but most are still alert and responsive when food is in the offing. Let's take advantage of it.

No more freebies! Treats are now an interactive food source. The dog has to do something to get the treat. The food need not be special. In fact, some dogs consume their everyday ration of chow divided up into training rewards. Dogs that are used to eating dry kibble often enjoy semi-moist food as a training treat—the type that looks like pieces of "real" meat and comes in foil-sealed packages. Soft foods don't need much chewing and are less apt to crumble, fall to the floor and distract your dog from the task at hand as he snuffles along.

If your dog has a food allergy, remember that when considering training treats. Some breeds have problems with high protein levels. Some dogs can't tolerate extra fat. Check with your veterinarian about training treats.

Sometimes a special food treat is preferred. Favorite commercially prepared options include:

- Freeze-dried liver, if it's not too hard.

- Soft, grain-based treats. Jackpot! is the brand name of an all-natural treat that is the consistency of a soft gingerbread cookie rather than a hard biscuit. It comes in strips that you can hide in your hand and pinch off bits as needed.

A few of my favorite homemade training treats are:

- Low-fat mozzarella cheese cut into eighth-inch cubes. Sometimes you can find it in stick form. Simply slice off little circles, or hold it in your hand and pinch off pieces as needed. Refrigerate.

- Liver treats can be made by boiling sliced calf's liver and drying it on a grate in the oven at 300 degrees F. Turn your oven off after 30 minutes, but leave the liver in for another 30 minutes, then cut it into eighth-inch cubes. Freeze or refrigerate. Unlike cheese, liver at least will always be in the refrigerator when you're looking for it. No one else will take it!

- Thinly sliced turkey franks are an alternative to liver. After you slice them, microwave until firm. Refrigerate.

- An occasional raisin is OK for dogs with a sweet tooth, but not too many. They expand in the stomach.

If you use human food, common sense prevails. Care must be taken not to unbalance *any* dog's diet. Let your veterinarian know what you are up to. Cheese, liver, hot dogs and the like are not nutritionally complete and should not comprise more than 10 percent of the dog's daily ration, according to Christine Zink, a veterinarian and a specialist in canine athletes. See how many calories your dog is eating by looking on the back of the dog food package, and then compute the calories in the food treat to determine how much your dog can have each day. Put that amount into daily quota packages. You can make your package last twice as long by cutting the pieces in half. You might consider combining your dog's daily ration of kibble with cheese. Shake it up together in an airtight container, and you'll have chow that now tastes and smells of cheese.

What About Toys as a Reward?

A special toy that you, not the dog, keep can be brought out at the right time as a training reward. One small enough to hide in your pocket or hand is the most effective. Your dog will play the lottery and never know if the payoff is coming or not. Even though the toy will be used interactively, be sure it's big enough to avoid the danger of choking.

Here are my favorite training toys:

Balls. A ball-crazy dog equals a great reward opportunity. Hollow rubber balls collapse and hide in your hand, to be popped into view when the dog least expects it for a quick catch or chase. Balls that squeak are especially interesting. The age-old favorite, the tennis ball, can be ready in a clip on your belt or in your pocket to be thrown for a job well done.

Foxtails. A ball with a colorful nylon ripstop tail, the foxtail makes it easy to control the dog and the ball at the same time. Hide it in your jacket or up your sleeve and whip it out by the tail to launch for your dog. The tail fluttering in flight really excites dogs.

Houston Chews. A short length of cotton rope with a rubber ball tied in the middle, these will fit in your pocket or hip pack to be brought out and tossed or tugged for a job well done. Houston Chews, made by Permanot, are safe to leave with your dog for a few seconds to chew and mouth. Beware of poorly made rope toys that fall apart quickly.

Squeakers. Some dogs just cannot resist a squeak toy. My favorites are three-inch discs that can slip easily in and out of your pocket. Your hand can fold over it so your dog never knows if you have the squeaker or not. The shiny eyes and furlike coat of a mouse squeaker fascinate lots of dogs. Round ball-like animals such as pigs or hedgehogs appeal to ball-crazy dogs that also like the squeak and beady eyes of a prey object. All of these can be easily concealed in your hand.

Work at building interest in the toy. Put it up on a shelf or in your pocket, admire it in view of your dog, then put it back. Talk to the toy, tempt your dog with it, put it back. What we really want is for the dog to be interested in you, so you should always be a part of this game.

The problem with toys is, unlike food, you eventually have to take them away from the dog. But if you're ALPHAbetizing yourself, your dog should accept this calmly and naturally. You'll find resources for toys and treats in Appendix A.

A list of your dog's rewards is an important first tool in your training program. Maggie's family has prepared a list of her favorite rewards, divided into three categories and in order of her preference.

Food

1. Freeze-dried liver
2. Low-fat mozzarella cheese
3. Moist grain-based treats
4. Semi-moist dog food

Toys

1. Disc squeaker
2. Ball on a rope
3. Pig squeaker
4. Furry mouse

Activities

1. Tug
2. Go for a walk or ride
3. Pats and praise
4. Fetch

TRAINING ATTIRE

The Human

Pockets! Maggie's human will need ready access to the rewards. Good dog trainers select their wardrobe not for style, but for the size of the pockets. The timing of rewards is critical—you might find a hip pack or apron more convenient than pockets in your shirt or pants. Some trainers wear a fishing vest, the kind with lots of little pockets, and others invest in treat pouches made especially for trainers. The type with a spring-loaded hinge closure is the best. Just a tap with your elbow will shut it, so you can stoop over without spilling the treats.

The Dog

Collar and leash. Sounds simple. It's not. In days gone by, the term *choke chain* was synonymous with obedience training. Recently more trainers are going by the motto "Use brains, not chains," meaning there are ways to train dogs that don't rely on brute strength. Your dog will need a collar and leash as a safety measure more than as an aid to training, because it's not necessary to jerk and pull your dog into position. Many dogs and most puppies will respond very nicely on their buckle collars. However, there may be a problem of security with buckle collars. You must find the right balance between being snug enough so the dog can't back up and pull out of it and loose enough to be comfortable.

A good alternative is a collar that restricts slightly when tension is placed on it, preventing a dog from pulling free. Premier is a brand name for collars known generically as half checks or martingales. They're much safer than the traditional slip collar because they cannot restrict any farther than the safety loop. However, remember that almost any collar can get caught on something and present a problem for an unsupervised dog.

If your dog is big and rambunctious and loves to pull, you may need the added advantage of the alternative equipment described in the next chapter.

Your dog does need some form of identification should he accidentally become lost. Tags on the collar are a good start, but a collar can also get lost or be taken off. Talk to your veterinarian about microchipping or tattooing as an alternative form of ID, and then weigh the pros and cons and decide for yourself.

When it comes to leashes, a six-foot leather or fabric leash is the most versatile for training. It's long enough to allow you some distance from your dog when you are practicing Stays, but not so bulky that it can't be gathered in your hands for close work.

An automatically retracting leash is great for casual walks. Your dog is safe but has quite a bit more range to explore. The spring-loaded mechanism keeps constant pressure on the lead as the dog moves to and fro, lessening the chance of your dog stepping over the line and becoming tangled.

Your dog needs a leash, for safety as well as for training, but unfortunately many dog owners use the leash to yank and jerk their dogs into position. Not only is this unnecessary and disagreeable, but a scientific principle, thigmotaxis, makes this counterproductive. Leashes can work against you! Literally.

Slip your finger in your dog's collar and pull slightly. Does he move away from or into the pressure? Unless overpowered or successfully trained otherwise, dogs reflexively oppose force. You can see why your dog continues to pull on a walk! It's much easier to go with natural instincts than against them.

The Bridge: A Word That Marks a Behavior as Rewardable

Dogs learn best in black and white, not shades of gray. You need to help your dog clearly understand your meaning. *Yes* and *no* are more clear than *maybe* or *sometimes*.

Establish a clear message of approval. Most dogs have received generalized, random praise and rewards in the past. Praise for being good, for being cute, just for being there. That's OK, but we need to establish a new word that quickly pinpoints and rewards the behaviors we are teaching. We'll use the word *Yes!* It should be said in a clear and enthusiastic tone and not lost in a muddle of other words. A distinct Yes! is much more meaningful than the vague and lengthy, "Yes, you sure were a good girl."

We need to build power into the Yes! For the first training sequences, we'll need food. Top on Maggie's list is liver. We won't use that. Because liver is so special, it may be overly stimulating for this particular exercise. We'll save the very best treat for special purposes. If we start with liver, we have nowhere to go. Besides, it might make Maggie too excited to concentrate on learning. So Maggie's training treat for now is low-fat mozzarella cheese cut up into pea-sized cubes mixed with a portion of her daily kibble allowance. This will be her primary reinforcer.

Since you will eventually be training her to walk on your left side, use your left hand for this exercise. Put five pieces of food in your left hand, close your fingers around it and make a fist.

Make sure Maggie knows the food is there. Say "Yes!" and give her a piece, dispensing it between your thumb and forefinger. Yes! will be her conditioned reinforcer. It will soon have the same power as the kibble-cheese mixture because it will reliably predict the food. Don't solicit a behavior, but do be careful not to give the treat if your dog is jumping up on you, barking, mouthing your hand or anything else you don't want to reward. If inappropriate behaviors occur, ignore them.

A delay of a few seconds before the next repetition will make it clearer to the dog that Yes! is a distinct cue rather than a regular series of words. Do this exercise two or three times a day.

To help Maggie realize that Yes! is a powerful and consistent predictor of reward, change things around. Do the exercise in different locations and situations: in the house, on a walk, in the car, while you're watching television, while others are around. Begin to vary the interval between the Yes! and the food. In future exercises Yes! will distinctly mark the good behavior and promise a reward. As the training progresses the interval between the Yes! and the payoff can become longer and longer.

If your dog becomes too excited and doesn't give you an opportunity to reward an acceptable behavior, don't say anything. Ignore her and go away. Next time:

- Do the exercise after her meal.
- Do the exercise when she's calmer.
- Change the food reward to one lower on her list of preferences.

If your dog is not interested:

- Be sure to schedule training when she's hungry.
- Use a clicker instead of Yes! (A clicker is a little handheld device similar to the childhood toys that are called crickets. Clickers provide a novel, attention-getting bridge.)
- Train during a naturally active time of her day.
- Change the reward to one higher on her list of preferences.

Chapter 6

Basic Training Exercises

TEACHING SIT AND ITS APPLICATIONS

Sit is not only easy to teach, but it's a versatil exercise. Where trainers once pushed and shoved a dog into a sitting position, we now use toys and food to motivate and lure. My slogan, and the essence of your Sit foundation work, is: Control the head, control the dog.

Begin your training session when Maggie is alert but not overly bouncy or excited. Hide several pieces of food in your hand and get her attention fixed on one piece. When she's focused on it, draw your hand over her head, back between her ears. Her nose should be like a magnet following the food. As her head follows the lure in your hand, her balance will change and in a sudden burst of gravity, her rear will drop into a sitting position. Be quick with your Yes! immediately followed by food.

Control the Head, Control the Dog.

If Sit doesn't happen, don't worry. You haven't given her a command, so she hasn't done anything wrong. Just try again. Give her lots of experience at hearing her bridge word Yes! and receiving her reward in the sitting position.

Now let's put the Sit on cue. A cue is a verbal command or hand signal that tells the dog what is expected. It's important to use the cue *when* the behavior occurs, not before. Dogs need to be shown what action the word stands for, or they might make a wrong association. Consider this: Maggie is standing in front of you wagging her tail. You say, "Sit." Isn't the word *Sit* more apt to mean "wag my tail" or "stand in front of my owner," than "put my rear on the ground?" If you don't say Sit until it happens, there's no need to correct your dog. She hasn't disobeyed!

Once your timing gets good at giving the bridge Yes! and the food when she goes into a Sit, start adding the cue. Say "Sit, Yes!" and give the reward. You'll be surprised at how quickly the dog learns. This is the power of positive reinforcement. Within a few days, start your dog on a random schedule of rewards. Sometimes she gets the Yes! and food and sometimes not. Don't be in a hurry to test Maggie. She'll need a lot of repetition in many different situations before she's well trained.

The "Control the head, control the dog" method works to help the vast majority of dogs to sit, but not all. That's what makes dog training interesting. Some dogs will back up instead of sitting, and you might find it helpful to work in front of a wall or piece of furniture as a stopper. You can also use one hand to hold the lure and the other to gently fold Maggie's hind legs into a sitting position. A gentle tuck behind her knees works much better than pushing her rear. Most dogs simply brace against pressure. We want to go *with* the dog, not against her.

It's important to establish Maggie's happy compliance with the command Sit. It will be used again and again as the foundation upon which to build advanced behavior modification exercises.

TIMING THE REWARDS

When you are establishing a new behavior, start by paying her (Yes! food) within half a second *every time* the right behavior occurs. This is called a continuous schedule of reinforcement. Maggie will learn very quickly this way with minimal frustration.

Once Maggie is performing reliably, the reward is phased out to only occasional rewards. This is called a variable schedule of reinforcement. Maggie receives the reward intermittently and unpredictably. There's no set pattern. This is the best way to perpetuate a learned behavior. Slot machines are an example of a variable schedule of reinforcement. Sometimes they give the player a reward, sometimes not, but people still play in hopes of getting the big payoff. Intermittent rewards teach the dog not to give up and to be consistent in her behavior. It's the same principle that keeps people going fishing.

My husband will fish all day and not get a bite, but will return the next weekend and try again. Why? Because eventually something great will happen. Same with your dog. Teach your dog to play the lottery. There's always the chance for a big reward. Be fair as a trainer; don't take advantage of your dog and forget the payoff. Instead, watch for the all-time best behavior during a session and give the dog a jackpot: extra treats, then break off into a game. Something very special.

With rewards, we're talking about carefully putting in a marker for a good job. That's important, but don't forget generalized "you're the greatest dog in the world" praise, petting and playing around. There are times you will have to make yourself more interesting than a scurrying mouse, a passing dog, a child with a candy bar. Build that attention in ahead of time. You need to be as spontaneous and enthusiastic about your praise as you are clever and expedient with your bridge word. If your neighbors aren't talking about you yet, you're probably not appreciating your dog enough.

To keep Yes! meaningful, think of the word as a tank of gas. Every time you say Yes! without a treat, the gas begins to drain. Say Yes! more than four times without a treat, and the power is gone. This doesn't mean you should treat every fourth time on a regular basis. Remember the principle of random reward.

STAY AND RELEASE

Once your dog responds properly to the Sit, you may want to add Stay or Wait. This is actually redundant, because a dog can't be sitting properly and not staying! However, Stay will be a useful word in the future, and this is a convenient time to teach its meaning.

Because dogs communicate mostly with body language, many dogs respond better to hand signals than verbal cues. A hand signal to accompany the word Stay is placing the palm of your hand in front of the dog's face for a second, then returning your hand to your side.

Accomplish the Sit and Stay by keeping Maggie's head up, looking at you. When her head is up, the laws of physics are in your favor, and it's easier for the law of gravity to keep her rear down. Try this yourself. Sit in a chair and focus on a spot on the ceiling just above your head. Now try to get up. Careful! Don't lose your balance. You can get up, but it's difficult.

In the ALPHAbetize Yourself program I recommend that you teach your dog to look at you when you call her name in anticipation of something fun. Say

"Maggie" and use the bridge and reward. She'll keep an eye on you because she'll want to be ready to play when you are. If you stand very close in front of Maggie, your position and eye contact make it difficult for her to lie down. If you sit her against a wall, she's less apt to stand up.

Start with a brief Sit-Stay. Maggie should be helped to Stay only a few seconds and then released. Slowly become more discriminating when you use your Yes! and treat. Raise the criteria to Sits with eye contact, Sits that are still, Sits that are quiet—whatever you like, reward it. It's fine to be wild and crazy in your generalized praise, just remember to keep the power and effectiveness of Yes! by not mixing it up with other words.

The Stay period can slowly progress to about 30 seconds over a week's time. Don't get too ambitious with Stay. Don't fall into the trap of testing to see just how long Maggie will stay. In the beginning stages of training a new exercise, the important thing is to make Maggie successful and reward that success.

At first when practicing Sit-Stay, you will be toe to toe with Maggie. When she seems steady at that distance, you can take a small step backwards. If you're extending the distance, decrease the time. If you're extending the time, decrease the distance. Once you establish this foundation, you can start to build on the time Maggie stays and also her distance from you, but not all at once.

Try standing sideways to the dog, standing behind, go outside, mix it up so the cue Stay will generalize to all situations. When things get tough, increase the delivery rate of the rewards.

Having a release word teaches Maggie to hold a position until a different cue is given or she is released. A release word that means, "We're done, you can do as you like now" frees your dog from the obligations of the previous directive. For example, if Maggie is doing a Sit-Stay, you'll end the exercise with a word like Free or OK or Done. Choose a word that is different from any other word you use with her.

Don't fall into the habit of releasing Maggie from an exercise and then heaping on the praise. What are you reinforcing? Jumping around *after* the exercise? If you are working on the Sit-Stay, praise while the dog is in that position. After the release, say nothing or praise only slightly.

Tips for Training Smart

Don't bore your dog. Keep training sessions short. A few minutes (not more than five), two or three times a day are enough to make progress without overwhelming or boring your dog.

Practical Applications for Sit-Stay

Once Sit is established as a rewarding behavior, it can be used as a substitute for problem behavior. You can see in the following examples how Sit-Stay competes with and takes the place of irritating habits. Great! Now you can praise your dog in situations where you previously felt like punishing. What could be better?

Passing Through Doors. Dogs get excited about coming and going. The ALPHAbetize Yourself program suggests you make it a habit for your dog to Sit by the door until it's opened and not go through until invited. In addition to making things easier, it will prevent Maggie from dashing outdoors unexpectedly and getting into the street. You will also find it very convenient to ask Maggie to Sit at the door before you enter.

Sit at Your Side When You Stop. We want Maggie to be a well-mannered, accepted member of your community. If you ask her to Sit each time you stop while walking in the heel position, it will help keep her under control and out of the way of other pedestrians.

Sit at the Curb. During walks, when you need to cross a street teach your dog to Sit before you start across. Vary the pause before crossing. This keeps Maggie under better control in busy traffic and safer should a car get too close to the curb.

Sit for Attention. When visitors come to your house or if you meet someone on the street while walking with Maggie, take the time to help Maggie Sit before you begin to talk or before they pet her. At first this can be practiced at home with family members or friends. If Maggie makes a mistake and gets up or jumps on people, ask them to simply ignore her and turn away. What Maggie wants is attention. Make her Sit to receive their attention.

THE SIGNAL FOR WRONG

We know it's best to start training by rewarding Maggie when she's being good, but sooner or later we need to transfer the responsibility of being good to the dog. If Maggie makes a few mistakes, it actually enhances the learning process. It gives us the chance to turn a gray area into black or white. We are already clearly defining what's good with our bridge and rewards; now let's make it clear when a behavior is *not* worthy of reward. Maggie isn't exactly bad, she's just not right.

Let's establish a word that means "I don't want this behavior." Your tone of voice should not convey scorn at all. The word is delivering *information*, not punishment. The term marks an action that is not desirable. In a neutral tone you might say "Wrong," "Oops," or "Sorry." With my own dogs I use the one-syllable sound *At*. Don't say "No" or "Bad." These words are too common and besides, they have a different meaning—one that Maggie probably already understands.

Remember how Maggie was taught Yes! as a bridge to the reward of cheese or kibble? Once this is well established, At can be taught the same way. Hide several pieces of food in your hand. Be passive, neutral. Casually open your hand to show Maggie. If she tries to get some, tell her At in a matter-of-fact tone, close your hand and walk away. If she stays put, tell her Yes! and give her the treat. Don't run the two together: Yes, At, Yes, At. At first keep a little separation between them.

Even though you remain neutral, At training is apt to be a bit depressing at first, so be sure to follow with some sort of upbeat exercise that can be rewarded. And don't use At to mark behaviors until Maggie has had a lot of experience with the above exercise.

Station Training

The concept of rewarding a dog for going to and staying in a certain defined area is called station training. It's one of the most useful tools in behavior modification and can be adapted to fit your particular needs. Maggie's family has decided they need a bit more control around the house and will use station training to attain that goal.

Here are the steps they'll take:

1. They've selected a small carpet as her station. They will use the word *Carpet* as the cue but could just as easily use another novel word like *Place, Rug* or *Spot*.

2. Maggie could be trained to Sit or Down on the station, or she could be rewarded for any position of her choice—Sit, Down or Stand—as long as she's at the station. Maggie's family will teach her to sit. They felt standing or allowing her to choose a position would not give them enough control. She's an energetic dog, so Down might be more difficult for her than Sit.

3. Several times a day someone will take her to the rug, say "Carpet" and help her sit if she needs help. As her rear meets the carpet, say "Yes!" then give her a reward.

4. The next step is to reward a Sit-Stay on the station with general praise while the owners walk away from her.

5. Next, put her on a Stay a few feet away from the station, go over and make a big show of dropping one of her favorite toys or food treats on the rug. Return to her and as you help her rush over and sit, tell her "Carpet." When she's there, "Yes!" and reward again.

6. Practice sending her from different directions and distances and start to randomize the reward. As she becomes reliable, pick the very best performances for the reinforcement: Don't reward slow go outs or a Sit on the edge of the rug.

Practical Applications for Station Training

Maggie is particularly excited when visitors arrive. Put the rug within sight of the door, but not close enough that it's unsafe or too exciting for Maggie. When she is able to run out ahead and Sit on the rug for a treat, start rewarding her with generalized praise for staying until released. Then it's time for *you* to knock on the door and pretend a visitor is there.

Before long, Maggie will be able to control herself when a real guest arrives. Seat your guest and when things calm down, release Maggie to greet your friend. If you need help to control Maggie during the learning process, refer to the box on page 41 that explains how to make a temporary waiting station.

Come When Called

Unfortunately, many dogs have a negative association with the word *Come*. My friend Karla gets her students thinking about this with the following exercise: Think back over the last few days. When did you use this word around Maggie? Make a list and then look it over and decide if Maggie would give the situation a plus or minus. Here's a typical list:

- Come! She was jumping up to get Granny's sandwich. (–)
- Come! She was wet and I wanted her to get off my bed. (–)

- Come! The kids left the door open and she was in the neighbor's trash. (–)
- Come! It's time for your bath. (–)
- Come! I had to get the Kleenex out of her mouth. (–)
- Come! It's time to go for a walk. (+)
- Come! Quit barking at the mailman. (–)

The odds of Maggie wanting to come the next time you call are not in your favor.

Come is not a substitute for a leash or a fenced yard, but it is a word that could save your dog's life some day. Therefore, it's vitally important to motivate Maggie to want to come to you. Chances are she's already figured out that you are in no position to make her come unless she's on a leash. Threats won't work—she knows you're not able to carry them out.

Don't be depressed. You may not realize it, but if you've started the ALPHAbetize Yourself program you're already laying the foundation to make Come work without even using the word. It starts with attention and leadership.

It's important to remember two points: (1) Never use the word *Come* unless you're sure the dog will come. This means you have to be a superb second-guesser, or don't call her unless she is on leash. (2) Don't call the dog away from fun or into a negative situation.

Now, let bygones be bygones and wipe the slate clean. Pretend Maggie is a puppy. You might even want to choose a new word. Don't use Here if you are using the word Heel; it can get confusing. How about Place or Close?

Start with something easy. Do you feed Maggie twice a day? Does she enjoy her meals? You have two built-in training opportunities you shouldn't ignore. Perhaps you've been "too busy" to train your dog, but I'll bet you've never been too busy to feed her! Even if she is right there by your feet as you prepare her dinner, quickly step backward a few paces as you put the bowl down and say, "Maggie, Come." This is a good time to put in the Yes! It will doubly reward the Come, and the result of Come (dinner) will reinforce the meaning of Yes!

Same with going for a walk. If she's in the habit of bounding over to you when you reach for the leash, add the word Come as she's approaching. You may find other times in your daily schedule to be an opportunistic trainer.

Exactly where will you put in the marker Yes!? Decide ahead of time the criteria for coming. Most pet owners consider it acceptable if the dog hurries in and sits close enough in front of them for a leash to be snapped on. Keep your goal in mind.

Most dogs cannot resist investigating if you move away quickly. When you call Come, either back up or turn around and run. If training outdoors in an un-fenced area, use your retractable leash for safety's sake. Before you go for a walk, hide something great in your jacket: a ball on a rope, a portion of the dog's dinner. Periodically call Maggie to you for a game or for part of her supper. This will help you maintain your appeal even though there are new and interesting things all around to explore.

It is wise to handle the dog's collar a bit when she comes to you, perhaps even snap a leash on, then immediately take it off and release her again. This way Maggie will learn that coming when called and the presence of the leash won't always mean the end of a good time. In fact it might predict the beginning of a good time. It's up to you to figure out what that might be. Go look at your list of your dog's favorite reinforcers.

Here are a couple of games you can play with your dog to make coming when called the *start* of fun, not the end.

Restrained Recalls

You'll need an adult family member or good friend of the dog to help you with this one. Have a ball on a rope if your dog likes to retrieve or tug, or some food in a plastic container with a lid if your dog likes food better. Be sure the container is large enough that it can't be swallowed.

Play indoors or in a fenced area. Your assistant holds the dog by the collar. (It might be easier to have a small piece of leather or rope attached to the collar. This tab needs to be big enough to hold on to but small enough that the dog can't step on it and trip as she's running. Make a tab out of the leash your dog chewed up as a puppy!)

Show the dog the prize, and run away about ten feet to start. Don't call her yet and don't tell her to stay. Turn to face your dog and holler "Come!" Jump around and be silly. When she gets there, open the container and give her the food or toss her the ball on one end of a rope toy. Play tug if she likes that game. Make sure the fun is happening right there in front of you. Opening the container will focus her attention on you as she waits a few seconds to be called, as will playing with the ball.

At first the prize produces the desire to come. Later the desire to come produces the prize; leave your dog without showing the toy or food—it's in your pocket or jacket or hidden ahead of time within easy reach. Call "Come" and, when your dog is right there, touch her collar and produce the prize. Vary the distances, the rewards, the amount of animation you use. And once in a while, go back to showing the dog that you have something for her before you call.

Note: If there is a chance your dog will resent being restrained and become angry with your assistant, play the Boomerang game instead.

The Boomerang Game

This one is a bit more advanced. Play indoors or in a fenced area using a toy that won't roll far when thrown. Your dog can do a Stay, or someone can hold him for you. Stand facing the dog, and call "Come." The idea is that just before he reaches you, you use your release word and throw his prize in such a way that he rushes right past you to get it. Again, coming when called doesn't always end the fun.

You can play this game with food or a toy. With food, use three pieces of aerodynamically correct food, big enough to see. Just as the dog gets to you, use your release word and throw the food by either spreading your legs and tossing the food between them—not a good idea if you have a big dog—or at the last moment turning sideways and tossing the food so he rushes past you. After he has a chance to eat the bit of food, call him again immediately from that spot and repeat the process, having the dog rush past in the opposite direction for another bit of food. One time out of the three, don't throw the food, but have him Sit in front of you for it.

With a toy, use two retrievable items, one of greater value (to the dog!) than the other. Call as above, and throw the lesser toy. Then call again, showing your dog the better toy. Your dog may bring the other toy with him or leave it there, I don't care. When he gets to you, have some brief play time.

Some dogs fall into the habit of playing keep away. They'll come, but not quite close enough for you to reach their collar. Spend a few minutes a day reaching quickly for your dog's collar. If he steps back, say "At" and go away. If he stays still, it's Yes! and be sure to have that treat ready.

An obedience class instructor in Oregon does this: The owners must clutch quarters in their armpits when they call their dogs. If the quarters drop before the dog's collar is touched, it means they reached for the dog, which is exactly how some dogs learn to play keep away. Give it a try! I call this exercise "It's the Pits."

Teaching Maggie to Sit when she comes is another way to control those keep-away games. Tell her to Sit when she gets to you. If Maggie needs help to Sit, you can guide her head back with a motivator so her rear drops into a Sit. Have her Sit for a few seconds, sometimes more, sometimes less. Keep her guessing as to what will happen next. Sometimes you will touch her collar sometimes, you won't. Sometimes you'll put the leash on, sometimes you'll release her to go back to what she was doing.

Don't abuse the command Come by expecting results before the dog is trustworthy. Calling a dog that's only partially trained and having her ignore you is counterproductive.

COMBINATION EXERCISES

A good way to squeeze in a bit more training during the day is to combine several exercises. Use everyday routines to help remind yourself to train.

If you work on the Sit and the Come exercises a couple of times a day, your dog should soon be steady enough to try a Sit-Stay before coming to a meal. Ask Maggie to Sit and Stay in the dining room or hallway. Leave her, go to the kitchen, but remain in sight while you prepare her dinner. Tell her she's good. When dinner's ready, call her, "Maggie, Come," and give her the dish. This is a big reinforcer for coming and a good practice for steady Sit-Stays. If she should get up, say "At" and quickly put the bowl in a cupboard and leave the room without saying a thing. Try again at another time.

Tips for Training Smart

Set your dog up for success. Motivational methods are based on your relationship with your dog and the attention you give each other. Be sure your hair is pinned back to make is easy for your dog to see your face. Do your hat or your sunglasses prevent eye contact?

Stop Pulling!

One of the most annoying habits owners complain about is the dog that pulls ahead on a walk. Energetic, enthusiastic dogs are the worst pullers. They need to burn off energy with a walk, but these rambunctious dogs are the ones that get walked the least—it's just too difficult and not much fun for the owner to walk a dog that pulls all the time. It's a no-win situation, unless you train the dog. In this section I'll define two different concepts for walking the dog: Let's Go and Heel.

Let's Go means, "I don't care much about what you do on walks as long as you don't pull the leash and make us both uncomfortable." Let's Go is used when no one is around who may be bothered by a less-than-perfect dog, and it's safe and appropriate to give the dog a bit of flexibility as to what she can do during the walk. Most pet owners want the dog to be able to enjoy life, sniff and explore while on a leash, and just be a dog.

When the Let's Go command is given, it makes no difference which side of the owner the dog is on. The dog can be slightly ahead or behind. There are minimal rules for appropriate behavior, except the paramount one: Don't pull on the leash!

Heel, on the other hand, means, "Stay very close to my side and give me your complete, polite attention." Heel is a more formal and precise style of walking that is appropriate when you need more control.

Suppose you are walking Maggie along the sidewalk with Let's Go. All of a sudden you see the entire kindergarten class walking toward you. They're laughing and skipping and they all have ice cream cones. Ask Maggie to Heel and you'll be able to get past the kids without her pestering them for the ice cream. They're gone. "Maggie, Let's Go." She can now safely revert to being a dog.

The important thing is to decide at any given time if you want Maggie to Heel formally at your side or to just meander around without pulling—Let's Go. It needs to be one way or the other. Too many owners slip into a gray area. Clearly request one behavior or the other. When you no longer need compliance, use your release word or cue a different behavior.

Training Let's Go

If Maggie forges ahead and creates tension on the leash, stop. She'll soon learn that she's not going anywhere if the leash is tight. Just act as if she were tied to a a post (she is, and you're the post). Don't say or do anything. If you don't follow her, she will eventually figure out that she's not going anywhere if she pulls on the leash. .

Many dogs respond and soon give up pulling with just a few days of this "stand like a post" treatment. Some dogs will need a little extra assistance. Here are some additions to the program that might speed it up.

- Some dogs, when they feel the leash get tight, will pull for a little bit and then turn toward you to see what's happening back there. That's when the post comes to life, and you become the most interesting thing on the walk—more interesting than a candy wrapper or straining ahead to get to some as of yet unknown adventure. Pull a ball on a rope out of your jacket and have a game, or just continue your walk with a happy, upbeat attitude and create your own adventure for your dog.

- Help Maggie release the tension on the leash by calling her name. Now you can reward her for a familiar foundation exercise—eye contact. "Yes!" then food. Then go on walking, preferably in a different direction. You are the leader. This either works very nicely or makes matters worse: Maggie may figure, "OK, I got it, I pull the leash, Mom calls my name, and we have a game." This is where a professional second guess comes in. If you're in doubt, try something else.

- When dogs pull, they generally set their feet, lower their heads and pull straight against the opposition. Hello! Wake her up with a quick unbalancing maneuver. Step quickly to the side and give a few nagging wiggles on the leash. Twisting your wrist back and forth is all that is needed. The sudden pressure in a different direction gets most dogs to give up pulling and rebalance. That's your opportunity to redirect the dog's attention. Just remember, *when the leash is slack* is when you reward your dog by suddenly becoming more interesting than the environment.

"It's raining, I don't want to go outdoors to practice." I really don't accept excuses like this from my students. I just give them a different idea to try out. Here are two simple alternative exercises that will help speed your dog's understanding of "don't pull" in the comfort of your own home.

Tie the end of Maggie's leash to a leg of your couch or a door knob. Get a cowboy to show you a hitching rail knot. Don't know any cowboys? Find a Boy Scout to show you a slip knot. If Maggie pulls on the leash, the knot gets tighter. If you pull the tab, the leash is released.

Now, sit down just out of her reach with an empty paper bag. She doesn't know it, but her favorite retrieve toy is inside. Most dogs will want to investigate. If not, become interested in the bag yourself; rattle it a little. Maggie will be curious about what might be in the bag. If she pulls to get to you, ignore her or say "At," remembering that At is not punishment, it's just information. If the leash is slack, "Yes!" and get up quickly, release the lead, and get out the toy and play.

For a variation on this, put a treasure on the floor about 15 feet away. A favorite toy, perhaps. Or buy a second-hand windup toy at a garage sale. Set the thing off across the room and invite your dog, on leash, to go over with you to investigate and have a game. You know the rules for getting there . . . does your dog?

"I can't take the time to walk the dog and stop every time she pulls, I'll be late for work. But I do want to take her to the park before I go."

This is a problem. During the training period, it's a bad idea to allow the dog to pull at all. Doing so puts her on a variable schedule of self reinforcement. "Is this the time my person will give in and let me pull?" *Dogs learn best in yes and no, not sometimes or maybe.*

Until your dog is trained not to pull, if you have to get somewhere in a hurry, use an alternative to get from point A to point B: Carry a small dog, drive a large dog or use one of the training aids described in this section: the Controlled Walker or the Gentle Leader. There are few shortcuts in training. However, these aids make life easier while you are in the process of teaching your dog good manners. If your goal is to simply stop your dog from pulling, try the Controlled Walker.

Manufactured by a dog trainer and a pioneer in the Australian Canine Good Citizen program, the Controlled Walker is a collar with straps attached that pass under the dog's front legs to form a harness-like aid that helps eliminate the stress and discomfort experienced on both ends of the leash when walking a rambunctious dog.

The leash is attached to a ring on the back of the collar. It's easy to use because the dog does all the work. The owner does not jerk or pull the dog, but simply holds onto the leash quietly and allows the dog to experiment. The dog will walk into the harness and stop when she feels tension. With gentle guidance, the dog can then be encouraged to walk in the direction the owner had in mind and is praised as if it were all the dog's idea.

There are other devices similar to the Controlled Walker also on the market. While the Controlled Walker provides one of the better fits, always check under the dog's front legs to be sure there is no chafing.

Some dogs take matters into their own mouths and chew and bite their leashes. It's another ploy for attention. Stay out of that game. For just a few dollars, a taste deterrent sprayed on the leash will handle the problem.

Training Heel

This position is more precise than the requirements for Let's Go. Imagine you are wearing a pair of jeans. Maggie's head should be roughly in the area of the outside seam and as close as possible to you, without touching. By tradition, most dogs are taught to heel on the left side of their owners. Your dog can learn to walk on either side by establishing one cue for left-side heeling and a different one for right-side heeling.

Some trainers view heeling as getting the forging dog back into Heel position. This is often done with a choke chain and a jerk of the leash. Taking an active rather than reactive position, you are trying to develop attention and teamwork instead. You teach the dog to start at your side and choose to remain there because it's a great place to be. When you move, no matter the speed or direction, the dog strives to maintain that position.

If Maggie has had experience pulling on the leash with you following behind, begging her (in vain) to Heel, choose a new word, and start from scratch. Some popular terms for walking at the owner's side are With Me or Side.

Target Heeling

The object of target heeling is for your dog to touch a target, the underside of your fist, with her nose. In this way you can draw her head into the proper position. The fist acts as a lure at first, dispensing a reward, but allows you to quickly transfer to a verbal cue, as you will see shortly.

Prerequisites

1. The dog should be sitting quickly and happily on cue on a random reward schedule and can do so in distracting situations.
2. The dog should understand the bridge word "Yes!"

The Target. Load your target fist with five pieces of food, placing one piece so that it is visible between your thumb and forefinger. While standing in place, move your hand around a little to be sure Maggie will follow your fist. When her nose touches it, "Yes!" and food. When the five pieces of food are gone, the first round is over. Do at least five rounds, or until she has the idea that she must follow and touch the target to get the reward.

Distractions. Do the same exercise in different locations, adding distractions. To be fair to the dog, it's important that you add distractions now so that she can experiment, push the limits, and learn in black and white what she's expected to do to earn the reward. Here are some reasonable distractions.

Get ready for another round of targeting (one round is five rewards), but put one piece of the food in your right hand. While Maggie is following your target hand, drop the right-hand piece onto the floor. If she goes for that piece, say nothing, but casually step on it so there is no chance she can get it. When she touches the target, "Yes!" and a jackpot—food, game, attention. Celebrate her cleverness! If she didn't notice the dropped food, start over and be sure she has a chance to see it and make her decision. If need be, use your information word At if she goes for the dropped bit.

Recruit an assistant. This time, instead of dropping a bit of food, your helper will approach and offer Maggie a bit of food or a small squeaky toy. If Maggie chooses to investigate it, your assistant simply closes his hand over the distraction. If Maggie is more interested in the person than the toy, the helper turns away and becomes uninteresting. When Maggie returns to the target, jackpot! (If she was interested in the toy, be sure to have a similar toy hidden in your pocket so the two of you can have a game. *You* are the one who gives her all the interesting things in life, and all she has to do is learn how to earn them.)

Target heeling can be taught initially off leash in a secure area, but after you experiment a bit you may find it better to tie Maggie's leash to your belt or buy a special Walking the Dog Velcro belt leash for this purpose. That way, you'll have both hands free while keeping her secure.

Walking in Heel Position. Start with a Sit in the Heel position. Show Maggie your target fist. Walk forward a step or two. It's OK to allow your dog to nibble, but don't actually give her anything until she's moving properly. Then say "Heel," take only a step or two more, then "Yes!" and food. Give her some generalized praise. That bit of heeling practice is over, but you can start again immediately after the reward. Sit and reward the dog occasionally during the heeling. This focuses her and controls a gung-ho dog's energy, but most of the rewards in this exercise are given for good walking in the Heel position rather than sitting.

Heeling sessions should be very short, only a few seconds or a few feet at first. You may not even use all five pieces of food in the beginning. Make it easier and cut out 50 percent of the problems by walking Maggie against a wall, curb or fence. You can even pull your couch out from the wall and heel around it. These vertical surfaces will help teach her to walk close to you, and the frequent, happy Sits will keep the dog from forging ahead. You can now see one of the most important applications of our motivational Sit. The time spent on that foundation exercise is about to pay off.

Proofing the Heel. As you practice, change things around a little to keep it interesting. Get away from using the wall as an aid. Add distractions in the same way you did for the targeting exercises. Pretty soon you and your dog will be a smooth team. Start adding about-turns, one way and then the other. Do left and right turns, fast and slow walking, until your dog unmistakably moves as if stuck with Velcro to your leg.

With small dogs, don't fall into the habit of rewarding while the dog is leaping. Reward for four on the floor only. At first you may have to stoop down a little to put your target at nose level, but you'll find the dog will be quite clever about assuming the proper position "long distance."

The Finishing Touches. Some dog owners are so delighted with the quick results of the Target Heeling method that they are hesitant to complete the training process. That is, lose the food. Well, not lose it really, but:

1. Your hand becomes an empty target. Food is now given from your pocket, or the dog is released and you both run happily over to a food cache hidden somewhere close by in the area. Change the location of this cache frequently: a shelf, a purse, a low tree or fence post.

2. Start to extend the interval between the bridge word and the reward.

3. You can use Yes! without food, at random, but no more than once in four times.

Another finishing touch is to transfer from your very obvious target fist to no target at all. The goal is for your dog to know where she should be in relation to your body with no target needed, much less food. Simply start to relax your hand out of a fist. Then change the position of your hand from Heel position to the way your arm normally swings when you walk.

You're there! Now let's practice. Here are some fun ideas to keep your lessons interesting.

Figure Eights

Pick two obstacles: chairs, bushes, whatever's handy. The distance between them doesn't matter much—four feet, eight feet—variety is the spice of life. Heel in a figure-eight pattern with occasional sits. The figure eight gives you an automatic increase and decrease in speed. It also teaches your dog to go around obstacles on the same side as you do.

The Spelling Bee – A Fun Way to Practice Heeling

Using chalk, draw some eight-foot-long letters on your driveway. Perhaps you'd like to spell out your dog's name. Maggie must Heel along the outline of each letter with you. Every time you come to an intersecting line on the letter, Maggie must Sit. You can use masking tape to make the letters when you're inside. You can always tell where my students live; they have letters mown into their lawns!

The Gentle Leader – Help With Heeling

While the Controlled Walker is a great aid in preventing pulling, the Gentle Leader gives more absolute control over the head and is therefore the aid of choice for heeling. It has applications for other exercises, as well. A professional trainer and a veterinarian joined forces to produce the Gentle Leader head collar. Another good example of creativity in dog training, it's like power steering—remember, where the dog's head goes, the dog will follow.

People have been using halters to lead animals for centuries. Which is easier, leading a horse wearing a head halter or one with only a rope around its neck? Similar to a halter, the Gentle Leader does not put pressure on the throat; it fits up higher and rests on the jaw bones of the dog. Put the side of your hand on your throat and push, then put the same amount of pressure on your jaw. You can see that the Gentle Leader has an immediate edge over conventional collars in comfort as well as effectiveness.

In addition to physical help in controlling the dog, the strap around the muzzle delivers a psychological message. In watching a group of dogs, you might see a higher-ranking dog gently encircle the muzzle of another dog with his own mouth. Leaders use this muzzle control to make a statement of rank. Most dogs recognize the muzzle strap as an extension of your leadership and will often settle into a more mellow attitude with minimal training.

Follow the instructions on the package carefully. Proper introduction, fit and use is of the utmost importance.

The Versatility Leash

You may have wondered about those leashes in pet supply shops that have a snap at both ends. I call this concept the versatility leash. You may want to experiment with one to increase the effectiveness of the Gentle Leader even more.

Snap both ends on the ring of the Gentle Leader, and bring one end around each side of the dog's head. You now have "reins" that give you more right-left communication power.

Or you can snap one end on the Gentle Leader and one on a Controlled Walker, and you now have control over the head and body at the same time.

Or snap one end on the Gentle Leader and one end on the dog's regular buckle collar for safety reasons. (Gentle Leaders that fit properly do not come off. If you're not sure about the fit, use a backup leash attached to the regular collar.)

DOWN AND DOWN-STAY

Down is a good control exercise and is a part of the ALPHAbetize Yourself program. Once your dog is responding happily to Sit and Come, work on Down. It may help to Sit the dog first. Get Maggie to direct her attention to your right hand, then drop your hand suddenly to the floor in front of her. If Maggie is attentive, her head will drop to see what's going on. If she's not attentive, a motivator in your right hand can be used to lure her down. Using the lure for teaching Down (and Sit) has an added advantage—the motion of your hand can later be incorporated into a hand signal for the exercise.

The rung of a sturdy chair can be used as an aid. Show Maggie the motivator on the opposite side of the obstacle. Maggie will have to get down low to follow the treat under the obstacle. You can also sit on the floor and use your own leg as an obstacle. As soon as she lies down, say "Down, Yes!" and deliver the treat.

Because Down is a vulnerable position, fearful dogs often worry about it and dominant dogs dislike it. While training this exercise, don't abuse Maggie's trust in you by asking her to lie down in a potentially worrisome situation.

While Maggie is down, praise her and help her Stay a few seconds with petting or the opportunity to nibble on a treat in your hand. Use the word *Stay*. Do not allow Maggie to get up until you use your release word. Down is not a punishment, it's just another position, so be sure to use a normal tone of voice when saying Down. Be sure to tell her how good she is with some generalized praise *while* she is still in the Down position.

Tips for Training Smart

One word – one action. Down means lie down. Don't confuse Maggie by saying Down when you mean Off. Off means get off the furniture or stop jumping up on a person.

The Emergency Down

This command can save your dog's life. Imagine that someone has left the gate open and Maggie is just about to run out in front of a car. If you've trained her to drop immediately into a Down, even from a distance and while on the move, you have a good alternative to Come and can control those situations and many others.

Start by dropping her while you stand in front of her (instead of by her side). Build distance. Don't allow even one step forward—the dog must drop on the spot. Tying Maggie to a stationary object will help keep her in place during training, or have her on a raised platform so that in order to creep forward she would have to take a step down. Reward her by going up and praising or by tossing a treat in front of her nose.

Another way to help with training the emergency Down is to drop Maggie while you are walking along, doing everyday things. In a cheerful voice, say "Down" and then immediately help her Down.

30-Minute Down-Stay for Visits

Maggie will be more welcome in your friends' homes if they know she will stay put when you station her and not get into trouble or get hair on their carpet. A good time to practice Down-Stay on the dog's station is during meals in your own home. But remember, the station needs to be a good place for Maggie—don't send her there as punishment. If Maggie's quiet on her station, praise her occasionally. Don't just wait for a mistake to give her attention.

Several times a week place Maggie on a Down-Stay. Make it easy by doing it during her natural lazy time. Your eventual goal is 30 minutes, but perhaps you'd be more comfortable setting a goal of 5 minutes and building up to 30 over time. A dog that has regular training for 30-minute Downs is usually willing to stay Down for hours or more on a visit. Whatever your goal, be sure your dog stays Down until the time is up.

The long Down exercise can be in conjunction with a regular task such as doing the dishes or reading the paper, but for now be sure you are in a position to help your dog stay Down for the predetermined time. You may need to stay with her, giving a doggy massage. You may need to keep a hand over her neck, scratching to encourage her to Stay. Remember, if the head stays down, the rest of the dog is likely to as well.

Praise Maggie occasionally while she's good. Remind her to Down-Stay if you have to. Over time you'll be able to move away from your dog during all of this. When the time is up, go over, praise her and release her from the position.

The Instructional Belly Rub

A belly rub is a good way to get your dog to accept and enjoy a subordinate posture. After Maggie has learned to respond happily and quickly to Down, once or twice a day invite her over for a belly rub. Don't bully her over. That proves nothing, except that you are bigger than she. We want it to be Maggie's idea to show you her belly so that you can rub or scratch it for her. Like muzzle control, this is just another part of your usual petting and stroking.

Some dogs quickly roll to one side in the Down position, so it's easy to start the belly rub. If your dog is the type that wants to lie in the sphinx position with belly down and legs under her, you can get her to roll onto her hip with a tidbit of food or an interesting squeaky toy. Put this motivator in front of her nose.

When she's focused on it, draw it along the floor toward her hip. If it's a high-ranking lure, her nose will follow it like a magnet. Her hips will turn, flopping her rear over into a relaxed position.

You can experience the mechanics of this for yourself: Turn your nose over one shoulder; now lower your nose over your shoulder as if you wanted to touch your ribs. Do you feel your hips rolling? When your dog's hips roll and she flops her hind end over on one side, there's a nice little pocket exposed inside her upper thigh. Yes! Start scratching there. Most dogs can't resist this and collapse on one side into a contented heap, belly in full view for a rubbing. If your dog doesn't relax for this exercise, don't force it. Just skip the belly rub and move on to another Down-Stay exercise.

Tips for Training Smart

Set your dog up for success. If you're going to practice Stays, why not practice when you know your dog has had a chance to get all the wiggles out and is in a calm mood. If you're going to practice Come, don't wake your dog up from a nap to do so!

STAND-STAY

Stand-Stay is another practical control exercise. Teach this after Sit- and Down-Stay, so that Maggie will have an idea of what Stay means. Start from Sit. With your leash or a lure, help her onto all four feet. Some dogs stand best if the lure is taken to their chest. They seem to want to pop up backwards to reach the lure.

This has the advantage of keeping your dog more or less in the same place without forward movement. It's easier for other dogs to simply walk forward with the lure at nose level, like a carrot in front of a horse, and then stop when the lure does.

When the dog's feet seem comfortable and still, tell her to Stand. The word *Stay* should not be necessary, but I find most pet owners are comforted by using that additional insurance word. Help Maggie Stay by controlling her head with the lure or leash and, if need be, controlling her rear by placing your hand and arm in front of her hind legs. To teach her exactly what Stand means, don't use the word unless she is perfectly still. Pay four-on-the-floor behavior with Yes!

Keep the Stand-Stay short and successful. Just a few seconds at first. Be very distinct about the release word and don't allow Maggie to move at all until it's given.

Practical Applications for Stand-Stay

Walks in the Rain. On wet days you may want to ask Maggie to Stand instead of Sit when you need to stop on your walks. It keeps her rear dry. Stand also puts Maggie in a convenient controlled position when you get home and need to wipe her muddy feet. This is behavior modification at its finest. Instead of punishing her squirming during feet wiping, train and reward a competing behavior. She keeps all four feet still until you lift one for wiping. If Maggie is being rewarded for four on the floor, she doesn't need to be punished for dancing around.

Grooming. Busy? You can brush Maggie twice as often in half the time if she stands still! Pinpoint times when she's very still and cooperative, and groom her at those times. Use the information word *At* if she starts to squirm. Only use At if you've actually done your homework and trained her to understand what it means.

Going to the Vet. Unfortunately, some dogs have a negative attitude about these fine people. If Maggie has made this association, don't ask for a Stand-Stay on the examining table, especially if you suspect that the procedure will be painful. The bad experience will just weaken the power of your Stand, not to mention your dog's trust in you. Unless asked for help, leave it to your vet, who has been schooled in animal restraint techniques.

SETTING YOUR DOG UP FOR SUCCESS

Train for a Good Response, Anywhere

Help your dog become reliable in all situations by varying the practice situation. Try not to change more than one aspect of an exercise at once. The typical variables for obedience exercises all start with the letter D: diversity, distance, duration and delivery of rewards. Change only one D at a time. And as you're increasing the difficulty of one criteria, decrease another. For example, if you are working on diversity, decrease distance and duration but increase delivery of the reward.

Delivery. Very early on in the training process you will want to randomize the delivery of your reward. Start to reward only the very best behaviors. If you're changing another D criteria, you may want to go back to delivering the rewards more often.

Distance. Increase this little by little. The dog comes when called if she is 10 feet from you. Now it's time to try moving a little farther away.

Duration. The dog is steady on her Sit-Stay for 15 seconds. Now it's time to try extending the exercise a little longer.

Diversity. The dog performs well in her usual, calm training environment (home, yard, obedience class). Now it's time to complicate matters a little by introducing distractions or taking her to a new training site that is distracting just because it is new. Will she walk as nicely on a slack leash in the park as she does in your backyard? Will she Sit and Stay in your living room if you walk to the closet and put on your overcoat? Will she Come if called while the doorbell is ringing?

Use It or Lose It

Dog training is a continuous process. In order to keep the communication channels open between you and your pet, constant refresher lessons are important. Just as the ALPHAbetize Yourself program becomes a way of life, so does training. You needn't put too much extra time into this. Find moments when your daily routine can be combined with a short lesson. If you have daily rituals, combine those with a bit of dog training. Here are some examples:

- Down-Stay while making the bed.
- Heel to the mailbox.
- Sit-Stay while you prepare the dog's meal, then Come.
- Station training while you brush your teeth.
- If your dog rides in the car with you, stop off at different places each time for a five-minute training session.

It's Got to Be a Lottery

Your dog's foundation of positive reinforcement needs to move from being continuous to being random. Only random reinforcement will ensure that your dog will do what you ask, whether you have a treat in your pocket or not. If you need help with the change, start by putting only three pieces of food in your pocket. Use those three rewards for the three best performances of the exercise you're training. Next time have five pieces, next time two. Mix it up. Some days don't have any reward except what you've hidden ahead of time in an easily accessible spot in your training area. Surprise your dog after an especially good segment of practice by running over with her to get the treat or for a game of fetch. This now becomes an even better lottery: Where is the reward? With the trainer? The tree? The shelf?

DOG OBEDIENCE CLASSES

The basic obedience exercises covered so far can be taught without the supervision of a training professional. What you've learned here is a beginning—a firm motivational foundation—but where should you go from here? You and your dog will greatly benefit from the guidance of an experienced instructor who can observe you both working together. The socialization value of a small, well-organized group class will help your dog have a positive attitude around people and dogs. You'll have the opportunity to learn new exercises and games, and maybe even get interested in competitive events.

Check on the reputation of an instructor before enrolling in his or her class. Find out what kind of training method is used, and make sure it emphasizes positive reinforcement. Appendix C has more information on locating and evaluating a dog obedience class.

Remodeling Inappropriate Behavior

The Untraining Tools

Most of the concepts we have explored so far could fall under the broad term of management. To set the stage for successful modification of problem behavior, always look back at the foundation blocks in the first chapters to see how your dog has been managed and make some adjustments, if necessary.

Make sure you consider:

H   **Health**—vet check, stress reduction, exercise

E   **Environmental enrichment**—home-alone hobbies, social time

L   **Leadership**—consistency, training appropriate behavior, ALPHAbetize

M   **Management in general**—common sense, supervise, confine, control

To help you remember this foundation as we goon to explore more specific tools, the acronym is HELM: Life with your dog is like a pleasant cruise, and you are at the HELM.

JOB-SPECIFIC TOOLS

Now let's take a look as some specific tools. A carpenter doesn't arrive at a remodeling job with just a couple of tools. He brings an entire toolbox full of them. He'll use one or two very often, most of them occasionally, and some may never make it out of the box. Each job requires a different assortment of tools. Your toolbox for remodeling problem dogs is a collection of ideas and concepts that will help you create your own approach to behavior modification.

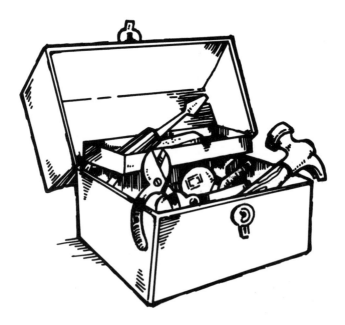

These are the tools you'll use:

- Yield a Little
- Eliminate the Cause
- Systematic Desensitization
- Take Away the Reward
- Reward an Incompatible Behavior
- Acclimate the Dog
- Improve the Association
- Negatives

Once again, an acronym might help: YES, TRAIN!

YIELD A LITTLE

- "OK dog, you can have your own piece of furniture, but stay off the others."
- "I can't walk you as often as you need, but I will hire a dog walker."
- "You can't dig in the lawn or flower bed, but I'll allow/train you to dig in this corner."
- "You can't get on the bed, except when I cover it with this old quilt."

Don't give in completely to your dog, but sometimes giving a little makes for an equitable living arrangement. Often overlooked as an option in dog training, a compromise can be an easy and effective solution. Yield a Little appeals to owners with little time, talent or inclination to train. Yield a Little allows the dog's preferred activity in a controlled context, where punishment might simply encourage the dog to pick another annoying habit.

As a tool, Yield a Little works well in combination with other tools. The main drawback is there might not be a suitable compromise available. Yield a Little is never appropriate for problems that might endanger the dog or those around the dog.

ELIMINATE THE CAUSE

- "Hello, Mrs. Jones? Peter is pestering my dog again. Please come take care of it!"
- "Are you growling when I pat you on the head because you have an ear infection? I'd better take you to the veterinarian!"
- "Dog, the shoes are now kept in the closet and I have the key."
- "You're destroying the house while I'm away at the office because you have too much energy? I'd better set up some activity for you before, during and after work."

Long ago someone told me about the KISS principle: Keep It Short and Simple. We might be overlooking a simple solution to the problem: taking away the cause of an unwanted behavior. Eliminate the Cause is quick and, when used appropriately, solves the problem forever and without stress to owner or dog. We must be sure, however, to correctly identify the cause. There may be a combination of causes or cues that provoke the behavior, and you'll need to peel them away like layers of an onion.

Bear in mind that Eliminate the Cause may resolve one specific issue, but may not change the dog's attitude toward other similar situations. For example, you may put your shoes away at home, thus eliminating the cause of chewing, but will the dog be tempted to chew something else? Better to dig for a deeper cause of the chewing, like stress.

SYSTEMATIC DESENSITIZATION

- "Dog, I'm sorry you're afraid of sirens. Today I'll play my siren tape for a little while. It will be so low you'll barely hear it. Tomorrow I'll turn it up just a tad. Then up a bit more, waiting to be sure you're OK with each step."

Systematic Desensitization is a technique frequently used for fear responses. The problem situation is presented to the dog at gradually increasing intensities. Critical to success is the owner's ability to control the dog's environment. Care must be taken not to proceed too quickly and overwhelm the dog.

Systematic Desensitization works very well with the tool Improve the Association. If you use the two in combination, the above scenario would be, "Dog, I'm sorry you're afraid of sirens. I know you love your food. We'll start very low, but during each meal we'll play the tape a bit louder."

Or consider this situation: "Dog, I don't want you to worry about walking on a leash, so I'll use Systematic Desensitization. First we'll just snap the leash on your collar and take it right off. Then we'll keep it on for a few seconds. Then we'll walk around the room and take it off. After that we'll go for a brief walk around the backyard."

If we add Improve the Association: "Dog, I don't want you to worry about walking on a leash. First we'll just snap it on your collar, I'll give you a food treat and take it right off. Then we'll keep it on for a few seconds while I pat and praise you. Then we'll walk around the room, go over to your food bowl and after you've finished your meal, I'll take it off. After that we'll go for a brief walk around the backyard and I'll toss the ball for you a little before I take the leash off."

TAKE AWAY THE REWARD

- "Dear, if you stop slipping the dog tidbits the begging will stop."

- "When you jump on me, I'm going to ignore you. You're looking for attention and my protests are actually more like fun than punishment."

- "Dog, I'll bet you think pulling on the leash is what gets you to the park sooner. From now on when you pull, I'm just going to plant my feet and stand still until the leash goes slack."

- "OK dog, from now on the trash is going to be very boring."

Almost all behaviors are sustained by a reward of some type. Sometimes the reward is subtle; you don't see it as a reward, but the dog does. Take Away the Reward is easy and takes little time or effort. The problem is that sometimes the reward is not obvious. Often there is more than one reward. If you can identify the reward with certainty and eliminate it, the behavior will eventually decrease and finally be extinguished.

Sometimes the behavior will abruptly increase immediately after the reward is withdrawn. This is known in behavioral terms as an extinction burst. In plain words, sometimes it gets worse before it gets better. If the dog is rewarded during this transient increase in the behavior, as often happens when the owner gives in, the dog has learned to play the lottery.

REWARD AN INCOMPATIBLE BEHAVIOR

- "You can't chew my shoe and your toy bone at the same time."

- "Here comes a child. Dog, Sit. Ha! Can't jump up, can you? Yes!"
- "Instead of barking for joy when the kids come home, go over to your toy box and pick up a ball. They'll throw it for you."
- "You can't annoy us at meal times if you're doing a Down-Stay on your station."

Train and reward your dog for a behavior that is incompatible with the inappropriate one. This is a very positive method, because the dog can now be rewarded for being good rather than getting punished for being bad. Instead of Bad for jumping, it's now Good for sitting. Instead of No for chewing the shoe, it's Yes! for chewing the bone. Rather than Hey! for barking, it's Good Job on the retrieve. Replace Shame! for begging with What a good dog! for the Down-Stay.

Reward an Incompatible Behavior reduces stress for all concerned. It does take time to train the good behavior, and you must be ready to reward it when it's offered. Then it's simply a matter of repetition until the dog knows when and where that behavior is expected. Chapter 6 will help you with training a good behavior that competes with the problem behavior.

ACCLIMATE THE DOG

- The Feel: "Dog, wear this collar. Get used to it. Nothing bad will happen; nothing good will happen. Period."

- The Look: "You don't like people in hats? You'll acclimate to hats because the whole family will be wearing hats when we are around you.
- The Sound: "Dog, I'll have to take you to the boarding kennel next week, so we'll listen to the CD they play in the kennel every day this week."
- The Smell: "Worried about the vet? Here's a carpet square from the office. It smells just like the clinic. Get used to it. I'll put it here at home where you have to walk over it every day."

Acclimation is especially helpful for fearful dogs or excitable, overreactive dogs. Often referred to as habituation, it simply means getting used to it. The dog is exposed to the problem-producing situation in a safe and controlled manner. The dog should be presented with neither reward nor punishment. Rather, through the calm and neutral environment the frightened dog discovers there's nothing to fear, the excited dog learns his antics will not be rewarded.

Acclimation is simple and requires little skill, but it can be time-consuming.

This technique may yield poor results with reflexive or instinctual behaviors. You must monitor the situation and stop if the dog is showing signs of stress, or you might make matters worse.

IMPROVE THE ASSOCIATION

- "Dog, I'll bet you'll change your mind about those noisy garbage collectors if I throw a ball for you each time they come."

- "Dog, I know he's wearing a white coat and stethoscope, but he's also got the best liver treats in town."
- "Dog, I'm convinced the word *Come* means run to you. We're going to start training over and use the word Here."
- "You don't like to ride in the car? Your last three rides were to the groomer, the veterinarian and the boarding kennel. But this month you'll ride only one block each day—to the park, where you can have a lot of fun."

Improve the Association, which behaviorists call counterconditioning, is one of the most widely used and successful behavior modification concepts for overcoming fear. It helps your dog establish a new, acceptable response to replace the fearful behavior. Improve the Association is useful when you can't change the problem environment. Pair something of high value to the dog—a walk, a chance to play ball, presentation of the food bowl—with the problem situation. The reward must be strong enough to overcome the problem, or else you might get the reverse effect: The reward will take on a negative meaning.

Negatives

- Sound: "The next time you try to steal dirty laundry from the hamper the motion-sensitive alarm will go off!"

- Taste: "You'll teach yourself not to chew up my magazines because I've applied a bitter taste deterrent to the covers."

- Smell: "Each time you bark, a little device in your collar will release a yucky smell."

- Sight: "Last time you were digging and scratching that spot in the carpet you got sprayed with my plant mister. I'll just put the mister near that spot on the carpet as a reminder."

- Feel: "My chair is not as comfortable for you now. When I leave home I place a metal cookie sheet on it."

Technically, Negatives fall into several different categories. But words and their definitions can be tedious. For our purposes, let's just say that we use Negatives to decrease or stop behavior because they have an unpleasant association. Some training programs use "corrections," which involve force or even pain. It's not necessary to go to extremes.

So far we've given lots of thought to choosing meaningful rewards from the dog's point of view. It's the same with Negatives: A squirt of water in the face may be unpleasant for one dog, while a Labrador Retriever might just ask for more.

The best Negative is one that the dog perceives as a direct result of his own actions, regardless of where the owner is or what the owner does. In other words, if the dog realizes you are involved, you become a conditioned punisher and the threat is only of value if you are present. Your absence signals all clear. If the Negative comes from the environment rather than from you, it is less apt to break down the trust your dog has in you. Therefore, carefully crafted "remote control" set-ups must be used.

Some warnings: Negatives are useful in only a small percentage of cases. If used at all, Negatives should only be considered with stable dogs.

Negatives can elicit or escalate aggression. If you correct a dog harshly, the dog may "correct" you back.

Negatives can elicit or escalate fear and should never be used on a behavior based in fear. If you punish a fearful dog for barking at the delivery person, the dog is apt to fear that person even more, and perhaps you as well.

Finally, Negatives alone are an incomplete regime. An alternative, appropriate response should be available to reward. Then the dog will know what *not* to do *and* what is acceptable behavior for the situation.

This book will cover some things you can do to improve your dog's behavior, but do consider seeing a professional behavior consultant. Appendix C will help you find one.

Chapter 8

To the Drawing Board

So, how do we put these tools to work? One of the biggest hurdles when working with a problem behavior is determining the cause of the behavior. If you don't consider the underlying reason, or if you get it wrong, you run the risk of not helping the dog or even making matters worse.

Why the holes? The dog might be looking for a cool spot. Yield a Little might work. Compromise by allowing the dog to dig in one particularly cool place.

The dog may be trying to escape. Why does he want to get out of the yard? Better begin by looking at Eliminate the Cause and go from there.

If the problem is too much energy and lack of activity, Reward an Incompatible Behavior would be a good tool. Buy the dog some good chew toys and praise him for using them.

It could be attention-seeking behavior. Do you go out to holler at the excavator? Better consider Take Away the Reward in your selection of tools. The dog has figured out an owner-recall technique.

The dog might be trying to bury or dig something up. Depending on his temperament, you might consider a Negative as one tool in your program. Perhaps rocks or chicken wire laid over his favorite digging spot.

The possibilities of combining the tools discussed in Chapter 7 are endless. From the digging problem, you can see that the tools are not always interchangeable or compatible. They are like pieces of a puzzle. You've got to get the right piece in the right place to solve the puzzle.

DOCUMENT THE PROBLEM

One way to figure out what's going on is to take notes. Place a notepad in a convenient, obvious location. Ask your family to help you by observing and documenting details of the problem behavior for several days. You might get a friend or neighbor to help observe your dog when you're not home, or try setting up a tape recorder or video camera.

Mr. Smith's neighbor in the next apartment has complained that Mr. Smith's dog, Fluff, barks too much. Begin solving this problem by asking a few pertinent questions.

When does the behavior occur? Is there any pattern to when Fluff barks? Does she bark in the morning, on the weekends or only after Mr. Smith leaves for work? By setting a tape recorder, Mr. Smith discovered that Fluff barks on weekdays only, in the mornings and in the afternoon.

What is the duration and intensity of the behavior? We don't know how long Fluff has been barking, because the neighbor only started complaining last month. The neighbor said she starts barking furiously at about 8:30 in the morning, tapers off to occasional barking and stops altogether at about 8:45. The barking resumes with high intensity at about 3:00 in the afternoon, dwindles and eventually stops by 3:30.

Where does the behavior occur? Is Fluff in the backyard when she barks or is she inside? The neighbor only hears barking from the front part of the house, the side that faces the street. Fluff is indoors, in the front of the house.

Who is present when the behavior occurs? Does Fluff only bark when she's alone? Does it make any difference who is with her? Since the problem was reported, Mr. Smith spent three days home from work on sick leave. Sure enough, he discovered that at the reported times, Fluff leaps from her basket and barks at the windows that face the front of the house.

What solutions have been tried? Dealing with behavior problems can be a process of trial and error. Since Mr. Smith just became aware of Fluff's barking, there hasn't been much time to try to stop it. He did try having the neighbor slap the wall with a rolled up newspaper whenever Fluff barks, but this hasn't worked at all. In fact, it has made matters worse.

Answering these questions about Fluff has led to some clues that might help solve the problem. It seems Fluff is barking at children walking to and from the school bus. When Mr. Smith adopted Fluff from the shelter, her card was marked "afraid of children." She learned that barking keeps children away and proves this to herself every day. As Fluff perceives it, she barks at the window at approaching children and they leave. Recently, her suspicions of children have been reinforced. Occasionally when they pass, a very loud crash is heard and it seems the wall is about to fall in on her. Documenting the problem has given us enough information to start building a program to help her.

Having a clearly defined plan of action is necessary to effectively remodel your dog. Setting goals and formulating your course of action will avoid confusing the dog and ensure success.

Build a House – Train a Dog

Step One: Goals

How do you want your house to look?

Exactly how do you want your dog to act?

Step Two: Techniques – How To

How do I build this? I need a blueprint.

What exercises should I teach my dog? How should I teach them?

Step Three: Assembling the Components

What supplies and tools do I need to build my house?

What skills and equipment do I need to train my dog?

Step Four: Implementation

Build the house.

Train the dog.

Step Five: Evaluation

Does the house pass inspection?

Does it look the way I want?
Is it sound?

Does my dog behave the way I
want him to?

Step Six: Modification

Fix the problems and improve
on the details of my house.

Select a different approach and
fine-tune my dog's behavior.

Goal achieved!

Great house.

Great dog.

Make sure your dog training goals are unambiguous. The carpenter knows he needs to put a roof on the house but hasn't thought through the problem: Will he used shake shingles or plastic tiles? Should the roof be pitched or flat? Should he put a solar panel in while he's at it? At times your dog training goals will be obvious, but at other times they will be vague. For instance, do you want Fluff to stop barking—period—or is it OK if she barks at a strange noise in the middle of the night? Is it OK if she whines? How about just one bark and then quiet? Each goal has a different game plan. Take a look at the flowchart on the previous pages, which compares behavior modification to building a house. When working with dogs, people tend to jump right in with steps four and five, only to find out they have to go back and consider one, two and three.

Of course, things don't always work out this way. You get to step five and your goal has not been achieved. Now what? Learn from that. If you try to help Fluff's barking problem by ignoring her and she continues, at least you know what doesn't work. Consider it not as a failure, but as a diagnostic step toward the solution.

LATERAL THINKING IN DOG TRAINING

You've been given some very specific tools to help you solve particular canine behavior problems. Your success at solving your own problems, however, may depend on how you think. Very simply stated, there are two broad categories of thinking: vertical and lateral. Most of us think vertically. We go from one logical step to the next, moving toward the one correct solution to our problem. It's a useful way of thinking, but it's not the only way. Lateral thinking is about changing patterns. Instead of limiting oneself to the usual pattern, lateral thinking encourages restructuring the pattern altogether.

Imagine you're driving along the road on your way to work. The options on your steering column are park, drive, low and reverse. What gear should you use? Everyone around you is using drive. You would never drive to work in reverse. No one does that—it's not the preferred or usual way. Nor would very many people be in low. On the other hand, you need low if you get stuck in snow and you need reverse for maneuverability or to get out of dead ends or wrong turns. There are times in dog training when you're going to get stuck, take a wrong turn or hit a dead end. You're just not going to get where you want to go unless you revise your plan and use something different. That's where lateral thinking comes in.

The Nine-Dot Puzzle

There may be a relationship between your ability to solve this puzzle and your effectiveness at solving behavior problems. Both require lateral thinking and creativity.

The rules:

- Connect all nine dots.
- You must use only four straight lines.
- You can't retrace a line.
- You can't pick your pen up off the paper.

Hint: Set no limitations. Dare to be different and break out of your preconceived boundaries. The solution to the nine-dot puzzle is in the Epilogue.

• • •

• • •

• • •

Chapter 9

The Right Tool for the Job

Let's meet some dogs now. They'll demonstrate behaviors people typically complain about. Perhaps some of the profiles will match your dog. We'll explore how to use the specific behavior modification tools discussed in Chapter 7 for each dog. To enhance your lateral thinking, read through all the profiles. If your dog is a digger, read through barking profiles, too. You might get an idea you can adapt for your digger.

As you read through the following, you can see that the owners of these dogs need to look back to the foundation blocks (remember HELM?) for some of the answers.

NOISY DOGS

It's normal for dogs to bark. Birds sing, cows moo, dogs bark. Too much, too loud and at the wrong times is a problem—for the people who live near the dog. Barking to extremes is a symptom of a deeper problem.

Barking complaints fall very roughly into six categories.

1. Attention Seeking: "Will somebody please pay attention to me!"

2. Separation Anxiety: "Will my special person please come back?"

3. Lack of Activity: "I'm bored; barking is my recreation."

4. Excitement: "Do I need a reason? I'm just having a blast!"

5. Offensive Threat: "Get out! I'll chase you off."

6. Defensive Alarm: "Get out! Don't come any closer."

Attention Seeking

The dog wants somebody, anybody, to pay attention. She barks, then pauses frequently to look and see if anyone is listening, at which time she might wag, circle, bow or look otherwise charming. A social, pack-oriented dog, the attention seeker may learn that digging and chewing also get attention.

Trinka is a bouncy, cheerful dog who is full of life. She's in the habit of barking for attention while Mark is on the phone. What tools can he use?

Take Away the Reward

Up until the phone rings, Trinka is quiet and receives no attention. While trying to have a conversation, Mark attempts to keep Trinka quiet by correcting her with the word *hush*. A correction? No, Mark must understand that he is rewarding Trinka by looking at and talking to her. Sometimes he even grabs at her to try to settle her down, so now she has an interactive game of keep away as well.

Most dogs like Trinka, who like to give their owners commands, will benefit from a leadership program. It sounds as if Mark is pretty busy; perhaps he should take a look at some of the environmental enrichment ideas in Chapter 3. Obedience training would help them spend more positive time together, as well as teach Trinka some manners.

ACCLIMATE THE DOG

Trinka turns on with the cue of the ringing phone. Mark could record random phone rings and play them as much as possible. He could make a couple of different recordings in case she has the pattern memorized and realizes she's being duped. Radio and television stations often have sound-effects tapes for sale, but it's important that Mark have a tape that sounds like his own phone.

REWARD AN INCOMPATIBLE BEHAVIOR

Mark might consider holding back some of Trinka's ration of kibble and placing it in a Buster Cube in the closet near the phone. He could give her this pacifier before she starts to bark. Now instead of looking to Mark for attention, she'll be coaxing the cube to give up its bounty.

NEGATIVES

Since Trinka is an outgoing dog with a stable temperament, Mark, in addition to training a substitute behavior, could have some negatives ready by the phone. A shot of water from a plant mister may put a damper on her barking.

Separation Anxiety

True separation anxiety is quite different from the attention-seeking dog that will settle for any type of general interaction from any person or animal. The anxious dog is overly bonded to one individual. Fortunately these dogs, which suffer greatly when their person leaves, are in the minority when compared to other types of home-alone problems. Their bark is frequently high pitched and frantic. If you set up a video camera, often you'll see pacing, drooling, whining, scratching, chewing or howling in the direction the special person was last seen or heard. The anxiety is usually at its worse right after the departure.

Janet and Max live alone. Max follows Janet everywhere, even into the bathroom. He barks when Janet leaves him alone and shows other signs of stress, such as drooling and licking his paws. His distress is worse on Mondays and after holidays.

A review of Chapter 2 would give Janet some ideas on how to begin a stress-reduction program for Max. Her veterinarian might be concerned about the licking, which could result in a sore. He might advise temporary pharmacological intervention to complement the training and to help Max calm down. Janet may want to ask her veterinarian about touch therapy while she's there.

Chapter 3 has some ideas about enriching Max's environment. Perhaps Max could be persuaded to take up a "hobby" to keep his mind on other things besides Janet's absence.

ELIMINATE THE CAUSE

Because Max is overly bonded to her, Janet should redirect some of Max's focus to other people, activities, toys. Janet should list things Max enjoys most. The list might include going for a walk, playing fetch, being fed a meal. Janet should then recruit a friend or neighbor to create a bond with Max by doing those things with him.

Janet should keep departures nonemotional by leaving quietly without apologies. Upon returning, she should walk in calmly and not greet the dog until later. These subdued arrivals and departures are an attempt to make the separation less dramatic. Any attention taken away at greetings and departures will be given back at a different time during the day. For at least 30 minutes before a departure Max should be totally ignored, to lessen the blow of Janet's leaving.

ACCLIMATE THE DOG

Janet might habituate Max to the departure cues. What alerts Max that Janet is about to leave? Picking up her briefcase? The jingle of car keys? Putting on her coat? Periodically, when he's *not* barking, Janet can jingle the keys, put her coat on and take it off, carry her purse around the house a bit. She should say nothing while doing this and just ignore Max.

SYSTEMATIC DESENSITIZATION

Another idea might be to systematically desensitize Max to separation from Janet. She could start by placing baby gate across an opening between two rooms, keeping Max on one side for a minute or so, within sight but ignoring him. If he's quiet, he should be let out and no fuss made. If he's noisy, wait for a quiet pause and let him out. Try again, but increase the likelihood of success by adding the tool of . . .

IMPROVE THE ASSOCIATION

Janet could make Max look forward to being apart from her. One way is to get the dog hooked on toys stuffed with food. She might get out a toy and start paying attention to it. Talk to it, pat it, fill it with food while Max is watching. Put it on the other side of the baby gate where Max can't reach it. Yes, this is teasing. Janet could then walk around as if she were getting ready for work, picking up her purse, opening the coat closet door. She could return to the toy in a minute or so, admire the toy again, pretend to eat it, all the while ignoring Max. Then put Max and the toy together on the other side of the gate and go sit down for a minute or two. End the exercise while Max is still engaged with the toy by opening the gate and removing the toy. Don't praise him for coming out. The toy was rewarding him for staying in!

Remember the four Ds of changing criteria that we discussed in Chapter 6: Delivery, Duration, Distance, Diversity. If the see-through barrier is working, the distance between Max and Janet could be increased or Janet could sit with her back to him this time. Something extra special could be in the toy this time. She might try the same exercise by going into the bathroom and closing the door. Janet should come out again within a minute if all is quiet. This has a built-in insurance policy because Max knows Janet has never spent eight hours in the bathroom.

Randomize the times spent behind the closed door. A breakthrough has been achieved when Max's quiet outlasts his interest in the toy. Janet could then progress to very short departures out the front door but come right back to keep Max guessing. The problem with all of this is that most people eventually have to be gone from home before the dog has totally overcome the problem. A friend of mine recommends leaving a smelly old jacket or shirt on the other side of the door to keep the dog guessing.

NEGATIVES

Negatives are counterproductive with a dog like Max.

Lack of Activity

The underemployed dog has lots of time and energy but nothing to do. Think of a dog's energy level as a pressure cooker. The pressure builds up and is then released by a valve. The steam comes out and the pressure cooker is OK again . . . for a while, until the next time it needs to vent. A high-energy dog with nothing to do is like a pressure cooker with a clogged valve. He has no choice but to release his energy in any way he can or blow up into a major bout of barking or other manifestation of his frustration. We could take the word *bark* out of this topic and insert chew, scratch or dig, and it could easily be the same dog, with the same solutions.

The bark pattern of a dog in this situation is monotonous, with repetitive intervals. The bark sounds flat and boring, except some dogs that embellish it with an occasional howl. The lack-of-activity bark is directed at nothing in particular. This is a good case for better management in general and environmental enrichment specifically.

Jacob isn't missing people or wanting attention. In human terms we'd say he is just plain bored. He has toys in the house but doesn't seem interested in them. His owner slipped home one day to spy on him. Jacob sits in one corner of the living room staring into space barking in a monotonous tone.

ELIMINATE THE CAUSE

Find something for Jacob to do. Some dogs need to be taught to play with toys. Make the toys come to life for your dog. Pick one up now and then and offer an interactive game. Make them more interesting. Jacob had no interest in a cotton rope tug toy that was lying around for months. One night after her dessert was interrupted by a phone call, his owner had the bright idea of spooning some of the melted ice cream over the frayed ends of the rope. Jacob has been interested ever since in his strawberry chew toy. If your dog needs something to do, check out Chapter 3 for ideas and then use some lateral thinking and come up with a plan!

Reward an Incompatible Behavior

Jacob is now hooked on a toy that rewards him for chewing instead of barking. We might also add a negative.

Negatives

The barking behavior may be linked to the corner of the room. Rearrange the room so there is no corner. Intrusion alarms (sometimes called an electric eye) are reasonably priced. One could be set up to screech at Jacob if he tries to go back to his barking station. Meanwhile, several flavors of cotton rope toys are awaiting him in other parts of the house.

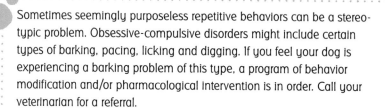

Sometimes seemingly purposeless repetitive behaviors can be a stereotypic problem. Obsessive-compulsive disorders might include certain types of barking, pacing, licking and digging. If you feel your dog is experiencing a barking problem of this type, a program of behavior modification and/or pharmacological intervention is in order. Call your veterinarian for a referral.

Excitement

This dog has uncontrolled high energy and lots of enthusiasm for life. Often self-rewarding, the dog is just having a rip-roaring good time, no further explanation needed! Things that wouldn't interest another dog arouse his curiosity. He's easily stimulated. His bark is high pitched and continuous. He moves around a lot as he's barking, is alert, wags his tail and often pants.

An excitable dog needs lots of foundation work. H for a health check is always in order. E for environmental enrichment goes without saying. The L for a leadership should included a healthy dose of obedience training to get all the wiggles going in an acceptable direction!

Oliver barks out the windows while he's traveling with his owner in the back of their station wagon. It's just plain fun. He dashes back and forth barking at things that move, so he might have a bit of prey-chase instinct keeping him going. The desire to chase is strong in many dogs, especially in breeds that were originally bred for such jobs. Oliver is rewarded for charging back and forth because he's successfully chasing everything away from the car. Every single telephone pole, person, dog, disappears quickly from his view.

ELIMINATE THE CAUSE

Rides would be easier if Oliver traveled in a crate draped with a blanket so he couldn't see the things that excite him. Include a toy to pacify him on the ride.

SYSTEMATIC DESENSITIZATION

Little by little the blanket could be removed. First open it a little toward the front of the car. That's least stimulating because Oliver can only see things coming toward him. Next try opening the back. Then, if all is well, inch by inch move the blanket to reveal the very stimulating sides of the car. Systematic Desensitization will work very well with . . .

IMPROVE THE ASSOCIATION

Convince Oliver that the car is no longer his private gym. Redirect his attention to a high-ranking chew toy.

TAKE AWAY THE REWARD

Oliver gets lots of attention from the driver when he's barking. "Hey you, shut up!" Oliver may just think his owner is cheering him on or at least barking with him. Take that attention away.

REWARD AN INCOMPATIBLE BEHAVIOR

Instead of whirling around the back of the station wagon, Oliver could be taught to Down on command. This could be rewarded by tossing a food treat or a series of chew toys in the back. For safety's sake, a passenger must help with this (so the driver can concentrate on driving). Or put the friend to another task: Oliver will have a hard time working up into a barking frenzy while lying down getting a full body massage. Start with practice in the driveway, then graduate to a quiet street until control is gained over Oliver's barking habit.

NEGATIVES

The same friend who's tossing the goodies into the quiet crate could also be armed. A beep from a light-weight boat horn might work. About the size and shape of a can of shaving cream, they're available at marine supply shops. Be careful it's not aimed toward the driver. Maybe a squirt bottle would be better!

Antibarking Collars

There are a variety of styles on the market. Some produce a shock when the dog barks, some an ultrasonic sound. Some models are prone to malfunctions. In general, the risk of physical and psychological side effects is great enough to warrant careful research before you consider such a device.

Citronella spray collars have been used with success. These have a sound sensor that triggers a burst of citronella spray when the dog barks. The liquid is a water-based lemon smell that is actually quite pleasant, but dogs find it disagreeable enough to learn quickly not to bark when the collar is on. Again, carefully consider the reason your dog is barking. Negatives are never appropriate for a fear- or stress-related problem. The dog must be trained and rewarded for an appropriate behavior. Never put an antibarking collar on a dog without an initial period of supervised use.

Offensive Threat

A brave, dominant dog protecting self, territory or possessions will bark at anything or anybody perceived as a threat. Displaying threatening intentions, this type of dog might carry through with the threat if all the variables are right. A lot of it has to do with critical distance, the imaginary circle around the dog. If a threat crosses that line, the dog feels something has to be done to get rid of it. The threat often begins with a growl and escalates into a bark. It's a startling bark of high intensity but short duration, which is great for the shock effect! See the description of an offensive dog on page 13.

Jazz is a brave, dominant dog who growls and barks to protect her territory, possessions and owner. Jazz has offered inhibited snaps at visitors. She's also in the habit of seeing off people and dogs who walk along her property's fence line. She's not so bad on walks, but her family tends to cross the street when someone else is coming along the sidewalk. She gets along well with her family, has been to obedience school and responds well unless she's too busy chasing off bad guys. Although she's never bitten anyone, her owners live in fear that she'll get over the fence.

Most cases like this need to be managed. A good place to start is with the foundation blocks of a health check and a stepped-up program of obedience and leadership. Take a look at the environment and see if Jazz can find a better hobby. While a behavior expert can help, no one would guarantee the safe behavior of this dog. True safety lies in the stopgap management strategy of Supervise or Secure, outlined in Chapter 4.

In Jazz's case, supervision should be upgraded. Perhaps her owners would feel more in control if Jazz were walked on a head collar. The fence seems to be a problem. Is it high enough and strong enough? Perhaps they could erect an inner fence to keep her farther away from the sidewalk.

The owners should then launch a behavior modification program directed by someone who understands what makes offensive dogs tick. Make an appointment with a professional behavior consultant who will take a careful profile on the dog and then set out a course of action that will probably include Systematic Desensitization and Reward an Incompatible Behavior. The dog also needs to Improve the Association with perceived threats by a regime of counterconditioning. Negatives should be avoided, as they could simply make this dog worse.

Defensive Threat

This dog barks when frightened. The bark is a sharp, high-pitched alarm sounded in hopes the scary thing will go away. The dog may step forward, but then retreats to a "safe" place. The defensive dog also has a critical zone, but is more apt to increase it by backing up than by chasing the threat away. See the profile of a defensive dog on page 14 and then take a look at the discussion in Chapter 2 on stress.

Good management would dictate that the owners protect the dog from possible confrontations before and during a fear-reduction program. A leadership program may help the dog transfer some of the worry to his owner. Fear and stress lead to distress and end up making a dog physically ill.

Chinook is troubled when the mailman approaches. He alternately barks and lunges at the window, then backs up when the man approaches the door. He's very suspicious of the letters that are dropped onto the floor through the slot in the door. Chinook is ill at ease with most people, but he particularly worries about the mailman.

In deciding what to do with Chinook, his owners will explore the foundation blocks of HELM and start thinking about the specific tools of YES, TRAIN. Because fear can be debilitating, ask your veterinarian for help and make an appointment with a behavior specialist.

ELIMINATE THE CAUSE

The first course of action would be to temporarily get a box at the post office and pick your mail up there.

SYSTEMATIC DESENSITIZATION

What are the auditory and visual cues that predict the arrival of the postman? The sound of the truck and the sight of a uniformed man climbing the steps. Could Chinook's owner borrow a hat from the mailman, or get a hat that looks just like it? If he seems afraid of it, that's defeating the purpose. Just put it up on a shelf and gradually bring it closer to Chinook's favorite spots. Family members might wear it, then while wearing the hat the family could play some of Chinook's favorite games. Then again, maybe the hat has nothing to do with it. Try to figure out what does.

IMPROVE THE ASSOCIATION

Perhaps Chinook is worried about the fact that the mailman is putting things through the door. A good reason to have the mail held at the post office! Start putting other things through the mail slot, like dog biscuits. Of course, Chinook will know it's you, but you can graduate to having friends walk up with hats and deliver the treat.

ACCLIMATE THE DOG

Ask your mailman's cooperation. See if he will put one of your kitchen towels on the seat of his delivery truck for a day. Get it back from him and make it a place mat under Chinook's bowl. He might as well start associating the smell of the mailman with something good.

REWARD AN INCOMPATIBLE BEHAVIOR

Fortunately, more than half of the time, a family member is home when the mail is delivered. Chinook loves to fetch, so have his favorite toy ready. Go outside and slip a letter through the slot. Cheerfully rush in, his favorite ball in hand, and start playing. Get a neighbor to deliver some "mail" at the usual delivery times. As soon as Chinook sees someone at the door or hears the mail slot, start the retrieving. Make a big fuss over him, too.

MESSY DOGS

What's that on the floor? One of the most significant reasons dogs are banned from living indoors is inappropriate urination and defecation habits. When dogs soil their homes they are often relegated to life in the backyard. This frustrating and lonely existence often leads to other problems, such as barking, digging, escaping and howling—prompting neighbor complaints. Unhappy neighbors are often the final straw, resulting in these unhappy dogs looking for a new home—recycling the problem as well as the dog.

Following is a list of reasons dogs urinate or defecate in the house. The vast majority of the problems fall into the first category—poor training or management—but read through all the case histories because there may be more than one factor contributing to why your dog messes in the house.

- The dog is not properly trained or managed.
- The dog is not healthy.
- The dog is overly excited.
- The dog is marking.
- The dog is anxious (fearful, stressed).
- The dog is a submissive urinator.

Training and Management

Indications of incomplete learning or poor management may not be obvious at first. You may have thought your dog was house-trained, but you have actually trained yourself to accommodate Sparky's schedule and he has never really been put to the test . . . until now. On the other end of the spectrum is the unthinking owner who simply doesn't give the dog a proper chance to be good. Somewhere in the middle are the owners who have not carefully structured their program of:

- Supervision: "I'm watching; I won't let you make a mistake."
- Restriction: "You won't want to toilet here in your small play area."
- Duration: "Can you wait four hours now instead of three?"
- Variety: "We're in a hotel room now; treat it like home."

Where Should Sparky Go?

People tend to concentrate on where their dog should *not* toilet. Thought should be given to an appropriate toilet area, usually outdoors in a fenced yard. Select an area away from the general traffic pattern but close enough to be convenient. You might set aside a small area with bark or gravel. Scooping is easier on these surfaces than on grass. If Sparky will be taken to toilet on leash in a public place, it's imperative that you carry a plastic bag for prompt cleanup.

Unless you want Sparky to use an indoor toilet full time, it's best to skip paper-training and train him to an outside toilet from the beginning. Exceptions might include the very young puppy left home alone for long hours, an unvaccinated puppy, apartment dwellers with small dogs, and disabled dogs or owners. These dogs might be trained to toilet on newspapers over a plastic sheet, in a litter box or on commercially available disposable pet pads. A pup that will be left home a lot could be kept in an exercise pen. This enclosure is roomy enough to allow space on one side for his bed and toys and a place on the other side for a toilet area.

Getting Started

It's all in the management. Stack the deck in your favor. What goes in on schedule usually comes out on schedule. Regular meals rather than free feeding will help manage the dog's toileting pattern. Sparky will need to defecate shortly after each meal and urinate more frequently. Very young puppies might need to urinate as often as every hour or so, especially during active periods. Sparky should be taken to his toilet area first thing in the morning, after a play period or other stimulating activity, after naps and just before going to bed at night. By 12 weeks of age most pups should be able to make it through a seven-hour night if managed properly. Withholding food and water late in the evening will lessen the chances of a puppy needing to go out during the night. He shouldn't need water through the night, but you might feel better leaving a couple of ice cubes in the empty water bowl.

When the pup first comes home, set your alarm clock several hours early so you can escort your pup to the toilet area. As your pup gains control, slowly advance the alarm to your normal wake-up time. Don't necessarily interpret whimpers in the night as a need to toilet. More than likely, Sparky's just looking for attention. If you respond to each whimper with a midnight social hour, who's training whom?

At the toilet area, stay with Sparky until you get results. Keep him on leash and slowly circle the specific toilet area to keep him focused. If he doesn't toilet within four or five minutes, try again later. When Sparky does go in the right place, instantly reward him with his favorite game and a lot of praise. Don't fall into the habit of taking him right back indoors after toileting. He probably likes to be outside with you, and you could inadvertently condition him to take his time toileting so he doesn't have to go back inside.

While indoors, it's easier to watch Sparky in a small area, perhaps one room. Close the doors or use baby gates to block him from other rooms. Keep an eye out for sniffing and circling, which often indicates the need to toilet. After you take him out, let Sparky roam the house freely for a while. As time goes by and he becomes more reliable, he'll be able to earn access to more rooms.

Telling Sparky to Go

A verbal cue such as "Go Potty" or a cheerful "Do It" can be used while Sparky is toileting. In time he'll associate this term with the need to go, so you can use it when you're in a hurry. Choose a term you're not afraid to use in public! One of my clients hums a little tune to his dog on such occasions.

How Sparky Can Tell You

Most dogs fall into the habit of waiting by the door when they want to go out. For fun, you might teach Sparky to ring a bell instead. It's practical, and a great way to impress your friends, too. Sleigh bells on a strap are good for this and easy to find, especially at Christmas time. Or try going to a farm supply store for a goat bell. Hang it from the doorknob. (You might want to put a protective sheet of Plexiglas behind it.) Hold a yummy tidbit in your hand close to the bell. If you hide it in your hand Sparky will eventually use his paw or nose to try to get it out. As he does, ring the bell yourself, load on the praise, give him the tidbit and outside you go.

You can shape this behavior by using your bridge Yes! At first reward any slight move toward the bells. Once he's trying, reward only better and closer moves until he makes contact with the bells. Once he starts catching on, you won't need to bridge or reward each time. Reward randomly. Sometimes Yes! alone is the reward, but most of the time it's followed by a bit of yummy food. If you don't couple the Yes! with food often enough, it begins to lose its power. Better not to say Yes! at all in that case and use generalized praise instead.

Don't forget the jackpot! For the very best bell-ringing attempt each session, end in a game or something your dog considers wonderful, like a romp outdoors.

Like all other training, just two or three minutes is enough per session. If you prefer a nudge with the nose instead of a hit with the paw, simply ignore the pawing behavior and wait for a nose nudge.

What If Sparky Has an Accident?

If you catch him in the process of making a mess, a loud noise like the slap of a hand on a wall will, in most cases, stop the act for a second or two—long enough to hurry him outside to finish. Don't allow Sparky to watch you clean up because some dogs will do anything for entertainment or attention. Finish with a commercial enzymatic odor neutralizer and blot it in. Put the legs of a chair over the area until it's completely dry. This will help Sparky avoid the spot should some residual scent be beckoning. Vow to be more attentive and not allow another accident to happen.

Don't punish accidents. Punishment will only frighten and confuse Sparky. Spanking, rubbing his nose in it or exiling him to the cellar does nothing to help house-training and does much to damage your relationship. We can never be sure Sparky understands exactly what he's done wrong. For example, if he made a pile in the kitchen and you smack him with a newspaper, he has only a slim chance of associating it with the accident. More than likely Sparky will think it's bad to be

in the kitchen, bad to poop, bad to be near you or he'll wonder why you're in such an unpredictably bad mood.

The Crate: A Natural House-Training Aid

Dogs are inherently clean animals. If given a choice, they'll move away from their eating, sleeping and play areas to toilet. Keep an eye on Sparky if he's on the move. When you can't give him your undivided attention, you'll need a way to temporarily restrict him to a small area.

Just as parents have used cribs and playpens to help them supervise their human babies, you can place Sparky in a portable kennel near household activities when you're too busy to closely supervise him. Dogs are social animals, and relaxing in a crate in the family living quarters seems much better to Sparky than isolation by locking him in the bathroom, garage or cellar. That type of isolation is apt to make him miserable and will be counterproductive.

Crates are available in a variety of sizes and styles. Wire crates are collapsible and provide maximum ventilation and visibility. Plastic airline crates are sturdier, provide more privacy for the dog and cut down on drafts. The crate should be just large enough for the dog to lie down, turn around and sit when full grown. If an adult-size crate is too large for your puppy, it will be less effective because it allows room for a separate toilet area. Partition off one end with a box while the puppy is small.

The crate can be used for short periods as confinement when no one is home, but it should never be used as a substitute for taking your dog to the toilet area at regular intervals. These portable enclosures mean peace of mind, knowing Sparky is safe, comfortable and not suffering a house-training setback. Crates are small enough to be moved around the house, perhaps into a bedroom at night.

Older dogs, particularly, might need to be conditioned to the idea that a crate is a great place to be. If you're using a plastic crate, they come apart in the middle, leaving the bottom half looking just like a dog bed. Turn it into one for a few days. When you reassemble the crate, keep the door open at first and casually toss in a food treat or a favorite toy as you go about your business. You may want to serve meals in the crate, but don't close the door at first. Ask the dog to get in the crate, leave the door open, sit down with a good book and keep the dog company and pet him while you read. Dogs take readily to crates, especially when used at night in their owners' bedrooms.

Because we want Sparky to feel safe and secure in his special place, teach children not bother him when he's in hiscrate. You're apt to find that Sparky will go into the open crate uninvited when he wants to relax and not have to worry about household activities.

As an alternative to the crate you could place Sparky on a leash and give it to a family member, or the leash could be tied to a nearby doorknob or heavy piece of furniture. Consider a temporary waiting station, as described on page 41. How about putting a bell on Sparky's collar to alert you when he's walking around? A trailing leash will also help call attention to the dog's travels and help you stop him in a hurry. Be careful, though, because the leash can easily become tangled. Make sure you are always there to supervise when Sparky is on a leash.

Train, don't complain.
—*Jack Godsil*

Now let's take a look at some of the other reasons dogs might mess inappropriately and how you can use behavior modification tools to alleviate the problem.

The Dog Is Not Healthy

Clues to a possible medical problem might include sudden unexplained forgetfulness in training, drinking more water than usual, a puddle of urine in the dog's bed or diarrhea. If your dog is on medication, ask your vet if it's one that can cause increased frequency in urination.

Sheba just doesn't seem to "get it." Although taken outdoors regularly and supervised diligently, she continues to wet the carpet. Sheba is not well.

She must be taken to the vet immediately, and then it's all up to management. Hopefully, there will be an improvement after medical treatment. Until Sheba is better, keep her under closer supervision and take her out a lot more frequently. Give her better access to her toilet area and reduce her indoor space to a smaller area with absorbent papers. This can be done with a temporary waiting station, baby gates or a crate kept close to her family, not in isolation.

The Dog Is Overly Excited

Sometimes a young, high-energy dog will dribble while engaged in an exciting activity such as greeting people. Usually the dog seems not to notice and continues with the activity, but sometimes the dog will pause briefly to urinate. The dog's body posture does not otherwise change, as it does with submissive urination or marking.

Champ can't seem to contain himself when his owners come home. He dances around and wiggles his greeting, depositing little drops of urine all over the floor. The same thing happens when company comes over.

Don't forget HELM. M for management of this type of dog would include taking Champ to his toilet area when guests are due to arrive. If Champ's bladder is empty, there is less chance of dribbling. Keep a large, washable carpet at the door or other greeting places. H: Certainly, a health check is in order just to be sure all is well.

Yield a Little

Sometimes this behavior will be outgrown.

Eliminate the Cause

Keep excitement minimal during greetings. Avoid petting, eye contact or reaching over the top of the dog. Instead of enthusiastic greetings, turn away at first, putting your face to a wall or a tree trunk. Don't talk to the dog until things settle down quite a bit. You can follow this with . . .

Systematic Desensitization

Gradually give back some of the attention as you enter the house. Just a little at a time. Perhaps only a glance at first or a word. If Champ holds it together, slowly increase the greeting over long periods of time.

Reward an Incompatible Behavior

Teach Champ to Sit to greet visitors. Most dogs are less apt to dribble if they are sitting. He likes to retrieve. Carry a ball in your pocket and throw it as soon as you walk in the door, to take the edge off the greeting. Better yet, keep a container of balls by the door.

Improve the Association

Set up training sessions where Champ sits for a massage. Do this during periods when he is naturally quiet and subdued. You might want to add a quiet cue like "Easy, easy" or hum a relaxing tune while very slowly and gently rubbing and massaging his body. In time, the tune will be associated with relaxation and can eventually be used in stimulating situations, such as greetings, to calm the dog.

Marking

Being nonverbal communicators, the odor of urine is one way dogs define territorial boundaries. Usually the urine is deposited near or on an upright surface, frequently at territory boundaries where others might pass. Favorite places might include fence posts or shrubs along the front of the property or on front window curtains. As a gesture of dominance, a dog might mark the resting place of another dog or that dog's possession.

Urine marking can occur with both male and female dogs. Most frequently, it is the unneutered adult male that has a marking problem. Often the dog that marks is otherwise house-trained.

Sport is a two-year-old intact male. He's lifting his leg on the end of the couch, which is under the front windows. It seems he does this in response to a neighbor walking her dog down the sidewalk in front of Sport's home. Foundation management would include a trip to the veterinarian to ask about your options. Castration or other intervention might be in order. Neutering Sport may well improve the situation. One study revealed a 59 percent reduction in marking after castration. This can do much to improve Sport's overall attitude. That's H; E and L are important here, too.

Evaluate the dog's environment. Does Sport need something else to do or to think about? Perhaps a new hobby from Chapter 3 would help. A leadership program may convince Sport that it's not his job to worry about territory, and he will be more apt to turn this responsibility over to his owners.

Eliminate the Cause

The trigger for the behavior is a passing dog. Closing the drapes or keeping Sport out of the front room may eliminate the stimulus. Playing easy-listening music on the radio will help mask the sounds of passersby. If Sport is used to staying in a crate, you might want to crate him until the problem is addressed.

Talk to the neighbor and explain the problem. She has a dog, so she'll probably understand if you ask her to walk the other way around the block, at least temporarily.

Don't allow Sport to mark outside in front of the house. Make sure he toilets in a part of the yard that does not border trafficked areas or walk him away from the house to toilet far from home. This may reduce the desire to remark territory already claimed by him.

NEGATIVES

Place Sport's water bowl by the spot he marks; also his food bowl during meals. Since the behavior is linked with just one area, this may be enough to discourage him from his usual spot, buying you a little time to come up with some other ideas. On the other hand, he may just shift to a different spot.

Pet supply shops have sprays designed to keep dogs away, which seem effective with some dogs. Other dogs aren't deterred one bit.

A more direct negative is to rig up some Elvis Presley cans: you know, shake, rattle and roll. Drop a few pennies in an empty pop can and tape it shut. If Sport looks like he's going to lift his leg, say nothing but roll the can along the floor to his feet. It will at least interrupt him! He may not think of it as a punisher. If he does, you run the risk of his blaming the dog on the sidewalk for it. Some dogs will think the Elvis Presley can is a new toy and retrieve it for you!

Point of interest: In some Asian countries dog owners solve this problem by pinning a cloth diaper on the dog. It's reported that, being naturally clean animals, dogs quickly learn not to mark. I'm not quite ready to try this one.

REWARD AN INCOMPATIBLE BEHAVIOR

Put some of your doggy friends on the payroll. Ask their owners to walk them by the house while a family member is home. At first sight of the passing dog, Sport should be called to a family member, who immediately plays a game or delivers a treat. Not only is he deferring his watch to the leader, but it's impossible for him to lift his leg while he's racing after a ball.

The Anxious Dog

Anxiety can be caused by many factors, but often the stress of being left alone or fear of something in the environment can alter urination or defecation habits. There is not much more that can be said on this topic that I haven't already explained in Part I. Simply review those chapters with this specific problem in mind. Also, read the section on fearful barking. Just think "mess" instead of "bark."

The Submissive Urinator

As in marking, submissive urination is a statement. Sometimes young or inexperienced dogs urinate to show deference to a canine or human leader. This acknowledgment is done with subordinate body posture, sometimes to the point of rolling over on the back, avoiding eye contact, licking and drawing back the lips. It can be seen during greetings or while receiving praise, and is not necessarily associated with fear or abuse but may indicate a dog that is a bit insecure in the relationship. It may be outgrown as the dog matures and gains more self-assurance.

Polly urinates submissively. When the family comes home, Polly immediate drops onto her side and raises her uppermost hind leg. Unfortunately, when she urinates it gets all over her as well as the floor.

Eliminate the Cause

Take a look into Polly's past. Perhaps she's become distrustful of people because of gruff voices or mannerisms. Until she improves, people should not move quickly around her. It will take time to build her confidence. That can be done best with positive training of simple exercises. Teaching her some tricks would be a good idea.

Polly should also be ignored for the first few minutes after her owners come home. By all means avoid towering over her, standing in front of her, staring at her or reaching over her head or shoulders.

Systematic Desensitization

When you begin to greet her, do it little by little. First a glance, then avoid eye contact and simply speak to her. When you give a pat, stoop low and to her side while avoiding eye contact. Pat her under her chin or on her chest. Take your time about moving on to bolder gestures.

Reward an Incompatible Behavior

Teach her to Sit using the Control-the-Head method described in Chapter 6. Don't lean over her; squat down to her level. Tell Polly how great she is. Ask her to Sit during low-key greetings. It's hard to grovel and Sit at the same time.

IMPROVE THE ASSOCIATION

Change her mind about people. Try to show her how relaxed you are so that she can also relax. Breathe deeply, yawn, lower your eyes. In general, look bored!

NEGATIVES

Not appropriate here. Anything that even vaguely seems like punishment, even a cross word, will make matters worse.

OTHER ANNOYING HABITS

Digging holes in your flower bed, mugging your house guests, chewing up your Navajo rug, stealing Sunday dinner, jumping out of the fenced yard—the list goes on, but the solutions still require the same basic tools and some lateral thinking. It all boils down to finding out why the behavior occurs, then checking through the foundation blocks (HELM) and the toolbox (YES, TRAIN). Here, in brief, are a few more common problems and examples of how you can use the tools in your toolbox to remodel them.

The Mugger

Some dogs leap about, jump up, mouth and nudge people in greeting because they haven't been taught otherwise, and in fact have been reinforced for it by flapping hands, high-pitched voices and other kinds of attention. Occasionally these behaviors can be interpreted as a display of dominance, but most of the time they are a show of uncontrolled high spirits, plain and simple.

Leadership exercises and obedience training to get the dog's attention and compliance are a must. General management should also be looked at. Perhaps a light house leash and a Gentle Leader head collar might help with control.

With young dogs, try to Eliminate the Cause by getting down low for greetings. Usually the pup wants to lick at your mouth, a typical puppy behavior with other dogs. Most dogs want eye contact, so make it easier by stooping to the dog's level. If the dog persists, Take Away the Reward of attention. Turn to a wall, hide your face and don't peek. Conceal your hands in front of you to reduce the mouthing opportunity and don't make a sound. The dog might get a bit frantic and try even harder for attention, but he will eventually quit.

The longest holdout to date is six minutes, but most dogs give up within a minute or so.

When the dog settles, quietly walk away and greet your dog later, but in increments, first a hello, then maybe some eye contact. Too much too soon might turn him on again. Don't give your dog less attention, give him more, but be careful about the timing and think of what you are rewarding. Reward an Incompatible Behavior such as Sit or Stand. There's no way the dog can jump up and Sit at the same time. It doesn't take dogs long to figure out what to do when you come home.

For bouncy, exuberant but otherwise friendly jumpers, you can turn this into a formal program by inviting some dog-oriented helpers over for a party; a dog training party, so they have to wear dog-proof clothing. They can help you and your dog practice several things. The first is station training as explained in Chapter 6. The dog should be indoors, dragging a house line. The dog must Sit on his station when the doorbell rings. The door doesn't open until you get a steady Sit. Allow the guest to enter.

In Sit for Attention 101, the guest is given a paper bag with some dog treats in it. Help the dog Sit on the station for a hello, eye contact and a treat. If the dog gets carried away and breaks the Sit, the visitor simply walks away and ignores the dog while you help the dog back into a Sit. You have the leash, so don't allow the dog to follow the guest. The dog will soon catch on that sitting is what gets the attention and the treat. If you run out of guests before the Sit for Attention is automatic, have them file out the back door and come in again!

On to the next lesson. Sit for Attention 102 involves a few hearty souls standing at least 15 feet apart in another room. They each have a bag of goodies. The dog comes up on leash with his owner. No one speaks to the dog. Helpers are holding their bags up under their chins, rattling them, and can make eye contact with the dog. The dog is brought within range. If the dog jumps, the person with the bag turns away and walks out of range. The exercise is repeated with each helper. The idea is that sooner or later the dog will Sit without prompting. Yes! and the helper delivers the food treat. Smiles, praise and pats are OK, but use good judgment—the dog may not have the self control early on to maintain the Sit if too much attention is given.

When this is working well, go on to Sit for Attention 103. Now the owner and dog are outdoors. The owner says nothing and does nothing except hang on to the leash. The helpers approach one by one with their bags. The helper's response needs to be black or white: Turn sharply away and leave if the dog doesn't Sit; quickly reward a sitting dog. Same old story—reward the appropriate behavior, ignore the undesirable behavior. Little by little have the dog wait in the sitting position a few seconds until the reward is given. The owner may have to walk the dog around after each helper's turn, because when the dog catches on he may not even get up at all.

This sequence transfers the responsibility of Sit for Attention to the dog. You'll need to practice this once in a while, changing the location and the helpers, increasing the duration of the Sit before the reward is given and being sure to eventually randomize the reward.

Be careful not to use Negatives in this program. We want the dog to be polite, but not wary of other people. The owners, however, can make it uncomfortable if the dog jumps on them by grasping the front paws and not letting go. Dogs are not built to stand on their hind legs. Before long, most dogs will start pulling away from your grasp. Simply let him struggle a second or two. Be passive and ignore the dog for these few seconds, then release him and walk away. Some dogs will tend to mouth your hands as you trap the paws. Bitter Apple or some other taste deterrent on your hands will discourage this.

Negatives must be balanced by teaching the dog an alternative, appropriate behavior. He now knows it's no fun to jump up. Show him that he gets attention for sitting.

The Food Thief

Maybe she's hungry, or thinks she is. Perhaps she has too much time and energy and not enough to do, so foraging seems like a good pastime. Has she received attention for stealing food—perhaps a game of chase? It could be that she's just a food-oriented dog with a low threshold for temptation.

HELM: A health check by your veterinarian is in order. Is the dog's food meeting her needs? Is she on medication? Several medications have the side effect of stimulating appetite. General management might have you feeding the appropriate amount, but divided into more meals. Use supervision or confinement when food is within reach.

Yield a Little by hiding treats for the dog to legally steal, or find other pacifying activities as part of an environmental enrichment program (see Chapter 3). Eliminate the Cause and Take Away the Reward (the food) by thawing your roast out somewhere besides the counter and putting the candy dish somewhere besides the coffee table. Child-proof latches on low cupboard doors will prevent dogs from rummaging around for goodies. The cat's food can be placed up high where only cats dare to go. Or put the cat's dish (and litter box) in a separate room with the door propped open with a piece of wood, just cat sized. Tie the door tight against the wood with a string running from the knob to a tack on the door jamb. Dog smaller than your cat? A baby gate across the open door might work if the cat can get over it.

Stop chasing and scolding when you catch the dog with stolen food. It may just seem like a game to your dog. Instead, call your dog over and trade something else for the food. Then vow to prevent future problems with management and training.

Some appropriate Negatives might be a setup with a motion sensitive alarm. Or you can attach several Elvis Presley cans with long cotton thread to a yummy piece of "bait" placed on the kitchen counter. Your dog won't know there's a string attached and will think the sky is falling when the cans come crashing down. (Alarms are not a good idea if your dog is overly sound sensitive.)

Sometimes dogs try to get up on laps or tables when people are eating. Show the dog this is not much fun by trapping a paw against the table top or grasping it in your hand for a little while. You should remain neutral during this. Say nothing. Have a "Who me?" look on your face. The dog will either try to pull away or mouth your hand (taste deterrent on your hand will remedy that!). Let go in a few seconds, say or do nothing more, and let the dog figure it out. After a few seconds have passed, coach him into the acceptable behavior (perhaps sitting at his station) and reward that. Better yet, head off these problems by stationing the dog before the meal begins.

There are other potential problems with food-oriented dogs that you can avoid before they get started. Teach the dog not to be grabby when taking food from your hand by holding your hand very steady when offering the treat. Don't give it up unless the dog is very gentle.

The Chewer

It's natural, dogs chew. Thank good-ness, because I use hobby chewing as a substitute for recreational barking, hole digging and other more bother-some habits. He's teething, he's bored, he's anxious about something and chewing is a good displacement ac-tivity. However, chewing anything other than his chew toys can be an-noying.

Remember HELM. Health issues must be ruled out, such as dietary de-ficiencies and dental problems. Stress would fall into that category as well. Environmental enrichment, general management and Eliminate the Cause would involve simple concepts like dog-proofing the house. If she's hooked on Kleenex, keep the box out of reach and the trash in a covered container. The problem is that for many dogs the whole house is one big chew toy. Leadership in the form of obedience training will help you call the dog away from trouble and retrieve the taboo item from his mouth without a struggle. A house line on his collar will aid in this as well.

Relieve some of the discomfort of puppy teething by soaking a rope floss toy in water and freezing it for the pup. If he's started munching a hole in the carpet, rearrange the furniture and put a chair over that place. For the time being, you may need to crate the dog in your absence.

Yield a Little by selecting lots of fun, legal chew toys and putting them out on rotation to keep them interesting. Teach chew discrimination as a formal game: Good Toy–Bad Toy (a game described in Chapter 3) will Reward an Incompatible Behavior. The idea is that while chewing on a good toy, you can't chew on a bad toy, your shoe for instance.

Take all gray areas out of the dog's decision making by the use of Negatives as an adjunct to more positive methods. Bad toys can have a taste deterrent on them or be attached to a motion sensitive alarm or an Elvis can.

The Potentially Dangerous Dog

Uncontrolled displays of fear, standing up against the owner with growls and teeth, chasing cats, charging people and challenging confrontations with other dogs are just some of the behaviors that are potentially dangerous for all concerned, regardless of your dog's intentions. "He just wants to kiss you," won't cut it with a terrified three-year-old or her family, even if it is true. The child may be traumatized psychologically or physically by your dog's actions, no matter how minor the incident may seem to you.

It's great sport for your dog to chase the neighbor's cat, and your experience says he means no harm because you've seen that same cat rubbing up against your dog's legs many times. But what if the cat runs into traffic? What if the cat's owner falls and gets hurt trying to get her cat out of the tree? What is your dog doing roaming around off leash anyway?

The shy and fearful dog is a potential danger—to herself and to those around her—because aggression is a possible result of fear. Stress is at the root of many debilitating physical problems. Don't wait for your dog to become ill, work on her problems now. Besides, they're not just her problems. She may seem to be coping by withdrawing from scary situations, but some day she'll find herself in a situation where she feels she has to take action to protect herself, such as a snap or bite. Do seek local help for the shy and frightened dog and read more about this problem in Part I.

We wish inappropriate fear and its consequent behaviors had been avoided with proper selection, socialization or training. But now these dogs need to be placed on a program to be sure they, and those around them, are safe. Appendix C will give you ideas on how to get help in your area. Until then, stopgap management procedures should concentrate on avoiding problem situations and supervising or securing your dog. Your stopgap measures would include:

- The Cub Scout meeting is at my house tonight. The dog usually goes into the back room and shakes when the boys arrive. Scout meetings would be a good time for the dog to run errands with another family member.

- Our dog lunges at the neighbor's dog if we see each other on walks. I'm going to walk in a different neighborhood until I can change that behavior. I'd better use a head collar to give me more control, just in case we meet the dog.

- Last week my two dogs had a fight. I'd better not leave them home alone together, in case they get into another fight and hurt each other. I'll make sure they're separated.

- The dog is lifting her lip and growling when I try to get her off my chair. I think I'll just turn that chair over until I can get an appointment with the behavior specialist.

- Our dog gets out of control in the park if a runner comes by. Let's keep her on leash at all times now just to be safe (and legal!).

The Escape Artist

Most of the escape concerns I hear deal with the dog that goes over, under or through the backyard fence. It's usually when the people are not at home. In my opinion this should happen only once, and then you do something to forever fix this life-threatening situation. The following ideas are *in addition* to properly confining your dog. First, make it physically impossible for the dog to escape, and then do the following to make him happier in his yard.

Why do dogs want to leave the yard? Perhaps he needs to get *away* from the yard. The yard is bad, he needs to go somewhere better. An example is wanting to get away from a thunderstorm. The dog is afraid and wants to escape. He doesn't realize that no matter where he runs, he can't outrun the thunder and lightening. Or, he may want to go *to* something. The yard is OK, but something out there is better. It's trash day! A smorgasbord of food and toys. Or there's a friendly little dog out on the sidewalk beckoning your dog to come cruise the neighborhood with her. Perhaps he's overly bonded and needs to go look for you when you leave. The reasons for escape are many and varied: romantic intentions, the need to mark territory, challenging those he sees as interlopers, or the urge to chase moving objects like bikes or joggers.

Under H, take a look at the studies on the effects of castration on roaming behavior in male dogs. Most research shows a reduction. Ask your veterinarian for reprints of current veterinary journal articles on the subject.

We have to address the separation anxiety; that's covered in the section on barking in this chapter. If the dog is so athletically inclined, E, environmental enrichment for him might include signing him up for a dog sport that involves controlled, constructive jumping while you are working on securing his yard.

One of the best things you can do for your dog is to make his home and your attention more interesting than the outside world. Do take the dog for walks, but have a brief play session in the yard before and after and look for other suitable enrichment ideas in Chapter 3. L: Leadership and training a reliable Come and Down is a must, just in case he should get out again.

The most obvious M, management solution, is to build a better fence—one that doesn't have cross bars that help in attempts to climb. Pouring a few inches of concrete over some reinforcement bars in a trench along the bottom of the fence works well against tunneling and keeps the lawn trimming chores to a minimum, too. Some people use long, narrow patio blocks for this.

In Washington State, where I live, dogs tend to just walk out of their yards in the snowy season. Get some exercise and shovel the launching pad area. Some folks keep a roll of snow fence and strategically place an inner fence on top of the snow, so the dog would have to be a broad jumper to think about getting over.

Once you secure your yard, a pet door that allows him in and out between the home and the fenced yard is an option. Most dogs would really rather be indoors anyway. If there's a behavior problem that prevents the dog from being indoors, it might be easier and nicer for the dog to address *that* problem instead of the fence jumping.

If the dog wants to escape to mark territory, make sure during walks that you prevent the dog from marking bushes and posts along your property boundary so he won't be as apt to want to remark them. If the reason for escape is too much energy and not enough to do, Eliminate the Cause by redirecting the energy to a backyard hobby, such as a digging pit. Drain the energy pool by playing active games before you leave. Quit early enough so you have time to ignore and settle the dog before you go. Consider a dog walker, day care or other options.

The dog that jumps over the fence, runs around the house and scratches on the front door to get in has learned that you welcome him in joyously because you were worried about him. It's an easy way for him to get you to pay attention. But that's past history. I could tell you to Take Away the Reward by being passive as you let him in, but I'm assuming that you will not allow the dog to get out again.

Sometimes accidents happen, despite your best efforts. Just in case, be sure your dog wears a collar with ID and is tattooed or microchipped for positive identification. Teach your dog to accept strangers reaching for his collar. Family and friends can practice reaching and treating, reaching and treating. If the dog is afraid of thunder, backfiring cars or noisy trash collectors, or is aggressive with pedestrians on your sidewalk, he needs the help of a local expert to set you on a program of Systematic Desensitization to Improve the Association. There's no sense talking about Negatives, because your time should be spent figuring out how to prevent another escape.

The Furniture Lounger

I think dogs like to get on furniture because it's comfortable, it offers a better vantage point and they like to be where your scent is. A person once asked Rudd Weatherwax, the trainer of Lassie, how he kept Lassie off the furniture. Rudd's reply was, "I don't; Lassie bought the furniture."

First ask yourself if it's OK for your dog to share the furniture with you. By day I spend time helping people keep their dogs off furniture, and by night I'm devising ways for my geriatric, arthritic English Cocker to continue to get up on the furniture—footstool by the bed, cushion on the floor by the couch . . . On or off the furniture—it's a personal preference.

Some folks would say getting up on human resting places is a display of dominance, but I wouldn't jump to conclusions unless you are seeing additional signs of running for higher office, as outlined in Chapter 4 on ALPHAbetizing. On the other hand, if your dog gives you stony stares or grumbles if you attempt to get him off the furniture, do ring up your veterinarian for a referral to someone who can help you with this problem. So the issue is, how to keep your dog off if you want to.

Going through the toolbox, we come first to Health. Dogs, especially in their golden years, like their creature comforts. Be sure those old bones have a soft, warm alternative to your furniture.

Yield a Little: You can compromise by putting an old blanket over the dog's favorite chair. Let it be "her" chair. If she likes to look out the window or watch indoor family activities, be sure her chair is placed in the appropriate spot. If your dog enjoys making her bed—digging and scratching around to make a "nest"—put additional blanket or towel pieces in that chair for her to arrange. Invite her over to the chair for some attention. If she jumps up on the chair on her own, be sure to mark that behavior with your bridge Yes! While you're at it, teach your dog to jump up on cue. There will be times when you do want your dog to jump up on something, onto a bench for grooming and into the car, for instance.

If your dog insists on sitting in your chair instead of hers, you'll also have to teach her to jump down. Being able to ask your dog to get off without trouble shows good leadership. At first you can use a light line to help the dog down, or lure her with the promise of a toy, a walk or dinner. Attach a cue to the jump off behavior like Get Off, and then fade the lure or help but present a surprise reward when the dog responds to the cue. After a while you can use the cue Get Off to prevent her from getting on furniture when you see her preparing for the launch.

If you don't want your dog to get on furniture, ever, be sure and Take Away the Reward for doing so. If the reward is comfort, make sure furniture is not comfortable. Tip the cushions on end. Spray underarm deodorant on the furniture. Most dogs don't like the smell and consider this a Negative. Put some aluminum foil or cookie tins over the seats. Put masking tape on the cushions, sticky side up. The dog won't like the sensation of being stuck. However, you cannot leave the tape down when you're not home in the rare chance that she might panic if she gets stuck. Let the dog experience the sticky tape while you are home. Later, you can put the tape on the chair seat, sticky side down, safe side up! Wrap it completely around the cushion to secure it. The tape will still look and smell like before. It will take a pretty clever dog to discern at a glance the difference between sticky side up and sticky side down.

The Excavator

At the beginning of Chapter 8 we talked about various reasons for digging: to get out of the yard, to get cool, to bury something, to dig things up such as a burrowing mouse. Some dogs resort to digging as a displacement activity for other behaviors they cannot or should not engage in. The fact is, for lots of dogs, digging is just plain fun. Some breeds historically earned their living by digging and go at it with a tenacity that is hard to discourage. You're hooked on golf, your dog digs. If the dog needs to drain her reservoir of energy, digging is probably a better choice than barking. If you absolutely have to stop the digging, be sure to provide another hobby!

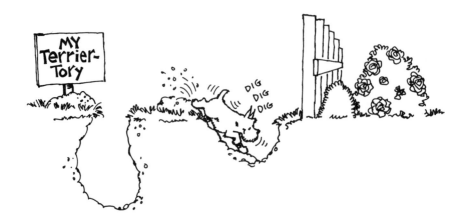

Looking at the list of why dogs dig gives you obvious solutions to the problem, most of which have already been discussed. Check "The Escape Artist" on page 158, for instance, if the hole is near the fence. Still, it helps with our lateral thinking if we go through the toolbox. Health? Well, female dogs sometimes have pseudopregnancies and dig dens. Not much you can do about that, but do check in with your veterinarian. Be sure the dog has something else to occupy her time.

Reward an Incompatible Behavior? If you don't like digging, select another hobby and redirect her energy to that. A spring ball might be an option. Check the section on environmental enrichment for other ideas. Be a good leader by using up some of that energy with regular training sessions and lots of exercise.

If she's digging, she's outside. Why? Most dogs are happier inside, or at least like to be given a choice. Train the dog to be good indoors and install a dog door.

Yield a Little! Compromise by fencing off part of your yard for esthetic beauty and part for a practical doggy playground. Find a suitable spot, shovel out the top soil in an area at least six by six feet and replace it with heavy sand. This makes digging easier and reduces muddy paws on a wet day. If she's digging to get cool, be sure to prepare a spot in the shade. The '49ers didn't dig just anywhere; they braved hardships of all sorts and *rushed* to dig where the gold was to be found. Make sure the neighbors aren't looking and then encourage her to dig in her sand pit by digging in it yourself and "discovering" her favorite tug toy or ball. Have a game. You can sneak out and bury things for her to discover on her own. A child's hard plastic wading pool makes a nice cat-proof cover for the pit and also helps keep it dry when not in use. It also doubles as another playground toy—just add water.

Negatives can deter the dog from digging in inappropriate areas: a sheet of chicken wire over a favorite digging place, a commercial dog repellent, a sprinkle of cayenne pepper. Some of my clients have rigged overhead hoses by threading them through tree branches. The nozzle points to the hole. Prime the hose and when the dog goes at it, turn the faucet on. Careful though—some dogs will consider that a reward. Landscape prime digging areas with river rock and shrubs. Pretty to look at, impossible to dig in and easier than mowing the lawn.

The Lonely Dog

Looking over my client records, lonely dog issues appear high on the list of the most frequently reported problems. The dog is usually presented as a chewer, a barker, a digger, an escape artist, but they're all manifestations of loneliness. Read over this chapter. In many (but not all) instances we can replace the word chewer, digger, barker or fence jumper with "lonely dog" and get the same basic formula for a remodeling program. Add the foundation information in Chapters 2 and 3, a good dose of lateral thinking, and you will be well on your way to improving the situation for your lonely dog.

The Perfect Dog

The only perfect dog is the one you buy from a toy shelf in the department store. Don't expect more from your dog than you do from humans. Sometimes even the most finely trained musician will play the wrong chord, and the most proficient typist will occasionally hit the wrong key.

Dogs are tolerant creatures. The vast majority will turn right around and lavish an apology on *you* if you should accidentally step on a paw. Surely we can meet them half way.

Chapter

The Finished Product

For thousands of years there has been a very special relationship between people and dogs—an interdependence. How did this friendship begin?

In his classic book from the 1950s, *Man Meets Dog,* Nobel prize–winning animal ethologist Konrad Lorenz envisions the relationship between humans and dogs as far back as the Stone Age. It may have started when a bored cave child raided the den of a wild dog-like animal and carried a puppy back to the family fire. "But Daddy, I couldn't help it, he followed me home!" At first Dad said no, but relented after he was barraged by a primal temper tantrum. The puppy stayed and the human-animal bond was born.

Today's people and dogs have retained the desire to share hearth and home. Our dogs are worth every bit of the effort we put into enhancing that relationship. It pays off.

To paraphrase modern trainer and behaviorist Ted Turner: "Dog training is like opening a savings account. At first you are making deposits only. But as time goes on the interest earned on your investment grows and grows. Sooner than you think, you can sit back and reap the rewards."

Epilogue

I didn't start out to write a dog training book. I'm actually too busy *doing* it to be *writing* about it. Most of this has been WIT (written in transit), thanks to my laptop computer, airline tray tables and a busy workshop schedule.

The document has literally been around the world twice. It's been pooped on by a noddy tern at the Great Barrier Reef (my R key has never been the same since) and left behind on a bench in Tokyo Station (my Japanese dictionary is still wet with sweat over this one). It went all the way to Switzerland and never got out of the suitcase (thank goodness for carry-ons with wheels!).

The project also survived frequent attacks of author displacement activity—you know, when cutting out Bonus Bone tokens for my next obedience class seemed more important than writing the next chapter. It's been through writer's block, computer crashes, deadline extensions and has survived two editors.

It's made me think about what I do, and why.

I hope you find it useful.

Here is the solution to the nine-dot puzzle on page 123.

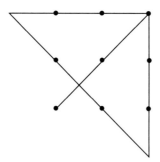

Appendices

Appendix A

Training Equipment Resources

The training toys and equipment mentioned in this book are available by mail. Send for a catalog:

LEGACY BY MAIL

Office Voice/Fax: (808) 871-0623
Toll Free: (800) 509-9814 or (888) 876-9364
P.O. Box 794
Kula, HI 96790
http://www.Legacy-by-Mail.com
LgcyMail@maui.net

Games for People and Dogs

In the main text, we talked about games for you and your dog. You can also have a dog party. Here some games the two of you can play with your friends.

MUSICAL CHAIRS

Place one chair for each participant in a line in the middle of the playing area. Alternate the direction the chairs face. Mark a rectangle around the chairs. The participants Heel around the line of the rectangle to music. At random intervals turn the music off and shout Sit or Down or Stand. Dogs must do so on or outside of the line and Stay while their handlers sit in a chair. Dogs creeping into the rectangle or dogs that otherwise break position must be repositioned by the handler. Everyone gets a chair the first time, but when the music resumes, remove one chair. When the music stops, the dogs assume the position the leader has designated. The handler who does not get a chair is out, but should be attentive because if a dog breaks position before the music starts again, the loser can steal that chair.

LASSIE SAYS

Instead of Simon, we have Lassie as the caller for this traditional children's game. Participants form a row, side by side with their dogs sitting in the Heel position. "Lassie says touch your dog's head," "Lassie says Down your dogs," etc.

GET A GRIP

Divide the group into two teams. Each team has a pair of chopsticks and two small bowls. The bowls are placed on the floor at the opposite end of the playing area on a place mat. One bowl has three marbles in it. The other bowl is empty. One, two, three, go! The first dog and handler from each team walks down to the team's bowls. The dog must be placed in a Down with nose or toes touching the place mat. The dog must stay Down while the owner transfers the marbles from one bowl to the other, using only the chopsticks. If the dog breaks, the handler must start all over with the marbles. Dog kibble is easier to handle than marbles, but you get too much help from the dogs.

SHOOT OUT AT THE OK CORRAL

Practice random Downs at a distance *à la* Doc Holiday. Two dogs and their owners are lined up back-to-back, with the dogs on a Sit-Stay. The Game Meister counts off as the owners walk ten paces. At ten, the Game Meister says "Bang!" and both handlers turn and cue their dogs to drop. First dog Down wins. Another dog can now come up and challenge the winner.

THE CHALLENGE

This is a good icebreaker. Dogs and people form a circle. Each person introduces himself and tells the group something his dog can do. (You can lie!) At any point, a player can say "I challenge." The owner must then prove it! If the dog can do it, the challenger leaves the circle. If the dog can't do it, he and the owner leave the circle. Keep track of the stunts—they can't be repeated by another player.

IRISH ROVER

Play some peppy music. People and dogs do the Irish Jig (dance or skip) to the beat. When the music stops, the dogs must drop. First dog Down leaves the floor. Repeat until only two dogs remain. The owners of these dogs have to clean up after the party!

PAR FOR THE COURSE

This is a recall from one line, across the "golf course," to another line. The dog should be in a Sit-Stay behind the first line. The owner stands behind the second line and asks the dog to Come. If the dog comes, she gets a hole in one. The score is one. If an owner is not confident in the dog's ability to Come, they can go only partway across the course, call the dog, leave her again, go a little farther and call. Each "putt" until the finish line is a point. Each extra call, each signal, head nod, and so on, is a point. The lowest score wins.

To set up an interesting golf course, create some diversions. See if the dog might get stuck in the rough; place a tray of tennis balls on the course. Or perhaps the dog might get stuck in a sand trap; place a kitty litter box on the golf course. Squirrels sometimes frequent golf courses; put a couple of stuffed animals on the floor.

THREAD THE NEEDLE

Place a number of hula hoops on the floor. Both handler and dog must go through all the hoops. This can be accomplished in a number of ways. The dog might be in a Sit while the hoop is brought over her head, or she might walk or jump through the hoops. Use your imagination. The team that makes it through all the hoops in the shortest amount of time wins.

PUT TOGETHER BY A COMMITTEE

For this one you'll need two identical plastic preschool puzzles with five to ten large pieces. Select two teams, dividing those dogs that can retrieve equally between the teams. Each team's puzzle pieces are set out across the room. Ready, set, go! Retrievers on each team take turns fetching a piece and giving it to the assembly people (the ones whose dogs don't retrieve). First completed puzzle wins. Award a penalty if pieces are munched. Note: If the pieces are dangerously small, put them in envelopes. Which is more fun—watching the dogs work or watching the assembly committee fight?

BOARD GAME

My Dog Can Do That is a fun new board game by No Guts No Glory, made for families and their dogs. Owners take turns racing to the finish line in Hollywood to take their position as Stunt Master, doing stunts (basic obedience exercises and variations on the theme) along the way.

The board game can be ordered through Legacy by Mail. The address is in Appendix A.

Legacy also offers booklets on games for dogs, written by Terry Ryan.

Appendix C

Behavior and Training Resource Organizations

When looking for an obedience class or behavior consultant, it's best to talk to your own veterinarian. Not only does your vet know you and your dog, but he or she also knows the quality of the services available locally.

ORGANIZATIONS THAT CAN HELP YOU FIND AN OBEDIENCE INSTRUCTOR

Association of Pet Dog Trainers
P.O. Box 385
Davis, CA 95617
(800) PET-DOGS

The National Association of Dog
   Obedience Instructors
Corresponding Secretary
729 Grapevine Highway, Ste. 369
Hurst, TX 76054-2085

What to Look for in an Obedience Class

Investigate—training classes are not all alike. Before enrolling, ask the instructor if you can visit a class currently in progress. Things to look for and think about before signing up:

- A good instructor will have a variety of techniques, most of them positive. Are the majority of the exercises taught by reinforcing good behavior or by punishing inappropriate behavior? Too much compulsion will have a negative effect on your dog.

- Are the people getting individual attention and coaching or is the instructor simply calling out general directions? A ratio of more than five students to one instructor is pushing the limit for a quality class.

- Are the instructor's directions clear to you? Do the people and dogs seem to be catching on with ease or are either confused?

- Is there reasonable control of the class? It should be clear to you right away who the instructor is and what is happening in the class. However, don't confuse enthusiasm and animation with lack of class control. A good class can have both.

- Can the instructor tell you the goals for the class and the steps that will be taken to attain those objectives? Are the exercises being taught useful for your lifestyle or consistent with your expectations?

Training class should be the highlight of your week. It should be a good night out with your best friend. Be brave: If you don't like what's going on in an obedience class, don't participate.

PUPPY CLASSES

Why wait and allow your puppy to fall into bad habits? You then have to untrain and retrain. Mold your dog to become a good canine citizen. As in human preschoolers, the experience gained in early puppyhood will influence the pups for the rest of their lives. Therefore, it's imperative that you check the credentials of any puppy preschool instructor. Here are some additional things to look for in puppy classes:

- The age groups should have a very small range. Young puppies, regardless of size, can be set back by the brashness of an older pup.
- Families should be welcome, but the class should not turn into a wild free-for-all. Children especially should be carefully supervised or pups could learn the wrong things about kids.
- Free play among small groups of carefully selected puppies is beneficial to their social skills. Care must be taken not to allow bully dogs to overly dominate the quiet ones.

Organizations That Can Help You Find a Behavior Consultant

Animal Behavior Society
c/o Dr. Suzanne Hetts
4994 S. Independence Way
Littleton, CO 80123
(303) 932-9095
shetts@aol.com

College of Veterinary Behaviorists
Dr. Bonnie Beaver, Executive Director
Dept. of Small Animal Medicine and Surgery
Texas A&M University
College Station, TX 77843-4474
Phone: (409) 845-3195
Fax: (409) 845-6978
bbeaver@vetmed.tamu.edu

American Veterinary Society of Animal Behavior
Dr. Laurie Martin, Secretary-Treasurer
201 Cedarbrook Rd.
Naperville, IL 60565
(630) 983-7749 or (630) 759-0093
martinala@juno.com

Association of Pet Behaviour Counsellors
P.O. Box 46
Worcester, England WR8 9YS
44-1386-751151
apbc@petbcent.demon.co.uk
http://www.webzone1.co.uk/www/apbc

WHEN SHOULD YOU CONTACT A PROFESSIONAL BEHAVIOR CONSULTANT?

Any time you feel you need help with your dog's behavior, but especially:

- If your dog growls, snaps, gives you a stony stare when you touch him, stand over him, try to get him off of a resting place or when you get near food or toys.
- If your dog lunges at or chases, nips or bites other people or animals or seems unduly afraid of anything in the environment.

When selecting a behavior consultant, look for one who:

- Uses mostly positive methods.
- Gives no guarantees.
- Sees your dog in person, not just a phone consult.
- Works with you and your dog, not a board and train facility.
- Doesn't misrepresent their credentials.

Index

TRAINING NOTES

TRAINING NOTES

TRAINING NOTES

TRAINING NOTES